The Wedding

ALSO BY DOROTHY WEST

The Living Is Easy

DOUBLEDAY
New York   London   Toronto   Sydney   Auckland

The Wedding

DOROTHY WEST

PUBLISHED BY DOUBLEDAY
a division of Bantam Doubleday Dell Publishing Group, Inc.
1540 Broadway, New York, New York 10036

D O U B L E D A Y *and the portrayal of an anchor with a*
dolphin are trademarks of Doubleday, a division of Bantam Doubleday
Dell Publishing Group, Inc.

Book Design by Gretchen Achilles

Family Tree by Jeremiah Lighter

Library of Congress Cataloging-in-Publication Data

West, Dorothy, 1909 –
     The wedding / Dorothy West. — 1st ed.
        p.   cm.
     I. Title.
PS3545.E82794W44   1995
813'.54—dc20   94–27285
                                                    CIP

ISBN 0-385-47143-2

ISBN 0-385-47915-8   (limited edition)

1   3   5   7   9   10   8   6   4   2

*To the memory of my editor,
Jacqueline Kennedy Onassis. Though
there was never such a mismatched
pair in appearance, we were
perfect partners.*

Love is patient; love is kind; love is not envious or boastful or arrogant or rude. It does not insist on its own way; it is not irritable or resentful; it does not rejoice in wrongdoing, but rejoices in the truth. It bears all things, believes all things, hopes all things, endures all things.

—1 CORINTHIANS 13:4–7

Colonel Lance Shelby
|
Gram (Caroline Shelby)

Old Sir marries Ebony Woman
|
Butternut Woman marries Preacher
|
Isaac marries schoolteacher

Melisse
|
Hannibal marries Josephine

Rachel - - - - Clark Cobb marries Corinne
(Clark's mistress)

Liz marries Lincoln   Meade engaged to Shelby - - - - Lute McNeil marries Della
| |
Laurie   Barbie   Tina   Maria
                                            by first wife   by second
                                                           wife (Polish waitress.)

CHAPTER ONE

*O*n a morning in late August, the morning before the wedding, the sun rising out of the quiet sea stirred the Oval from its shapeless sleep and gave dimension and design to the ring of summer cottages.

The islanders were already astir. There was milk to deliver to the summer visitors, stores to open for their spending sprees, grass to cut for them, cars to wash for them, an endless chain of petty jobs demanding preference, particularly in the Oval, whose occupants were colored, and inclined to expect special treatment.

The Oval was a rustic stretch of flowering shrubs and tall trees, designated on the old town maps as Highland Park. The narrow dirt road that circled it was Highland Avenue. But since in no islander's memory had there ever

1

been signposts to bring these ambitious titles to life, the area had long ago been assigned the descriptive name that better suited it.

A baker's dozen of cottages made a ring around the park. Some were small and plain of facade, others were bigger and handsomer (one, the Coles place, was called a mansion), and all of them were spruced up for summer, set back precisely on immaculate squares of green lawn.

They formed a fortress, a bulwark of colored society. Their occupants could boast that they, or even better their ancestors, had owned a home away from home since the days when a summer hegira was taken by few colored people above the rank of servant.

Though newer comers owned cottages in other sections of the seaside town, some very splendid houses in neighborhoods customarily called white, the Ovalites still outranked them. They had been the vanguard. They were now the old guard. It would sound like sour grapes to say, "So what?"

Even the label "Ovalite" had acquired a connotation completely the contrary of its original intent. For those who had bestowed it as a bitter epithet were now long gone from the scene of their failure to crash Ovalite society, and the name that was once profane had been sanctified by time and proper inflection.

The Coles house dominated the Oval. With its great glassed-in porches, against which many birds had dashed themselves to death, its ballroom, with the little gilt chairs that had hugged the walls for years now set in place for the wedding, and the undertaker's chairs in sober alignment, its sweep of lawns that kept the lesser cottages at a feudal distance, it was the prize piece of the Oval.

Behind it were acres of picturesque growth that had been part of the property in the baronial era of the first owner. Now they served as an effective backdrop for the Coles place, closing that end of the Oval to cars, making it a dead end.

The only means of exit from or entrance to the Oval was via a winding, rutted road. The underbrush on either side of this road forced one of two approaching cars to back to its starting place, a slow and tortuous procedure that often left scars on the polished hide of an oversize car that did not quite stay in the ruts.

The Ovalites could have followed established procedure and petitioned the town for a wider outlet to the highway. But this uninviting approach gave them a feeling of being as exclusive as the really exclusive—the really rich, the really powerful—who also lived at the end of impressively bad roads to discourage the curious.

The Clark Coleses came closest to being as real as their counterparts. They had money, enough not only to spend but to save. They were college-bred, of good background. They lived graciously. Two respectful maids had served them for years, living proof that they were used to servants. If Clark and Corinne had not slept with each other for years, even their daughters could not have demanded more discretion in their outward behavior.

Their daughters were Liz, the married one, and Shelby, the bride-to-be, both lovely, but Shelby lovelier, the image of

Gram in that tinted picture of Gram as a girl, with rose-pink skin, golden hair, and dusk-blue eyes.

That Liz had married a dark man and given birth to a daughter who was tinged with her father's darkness had raised the eyebrows of the Oval. But at least she had married a man in medicine, in keeping with the family tradition that all men were created to be doctors, whose titles made introductions so easy and self-explanatory.

But how Shelby, who could have had her pick of the best of breed in her own race, could marry outside her race, outside her father's profession, and throw her life away on a nameless, faceless white man who wrote jazz, a frivolous occupation without office, title, or foreseeable future, was beyond the Oval's understanding.

Between the dark man Liz had married and the music maker Shelby was marrying, there was a whole area of eligible men of the right colors and the right professions. For Liz and Shelby to marry so contrary to expectations affronted all the subtle tenets of their training.

Though Shelby might have been headstrong in her choice of a husband, at least she had let her mother dissuade her from following Liz's lead and eloping. Her wedding would have the Oval setting that Corinne had promised Miss Adelaide Bannister on a golden afternoon in her daughters' teens. Addie, breathing hard behind the bulging stays that tormented and squeezed the unsuitable flesh of her thin existence, had sat stuck to her chair on the glassed-in porch that drew the sun and made the heat hotter, fanning herself with the limp hand that waved in her face whenever there was nothing else to stir a breeze.

She accepted a brandy because it was medicinal, and the sun, and the too tight stays, and the brandy, gave her palpitations that made her bosom heave back and forth in a rapid way that always unnerved the spineless, who did not want to see her drop dead before them. Clutching her heart to hold it in place, she confided to Corinne that her greatest hope was to live long enough to see Liz married, not that she favored the older sister over the younger, but that it was beyond all hope that she would live to see them both as brides.

Moved by this sad and simple confidence and a very dry martini, Corinne made her sentimental promise that Liz would be married in the Oval, sparing Addie any tormenting trip to New York, where the unfamiliar place and people and pace might really cause Addie's untimely demise in the middle of Grand Central Station.

Since the day of her birth in Boston, Addie had traveled no farther from home than an island off the Massachusetts coast, a short and uneventful train ride, an even shorter and calmer crossing. In winter she rarely socialized, almost never stepping outside the old family house in Cambridge, where she swaddled herself in sweaters and bathrobes to rout the penetrating cold that battled the insufficient heat from the old-fashioned, dust-filled floor registers. Surrounded by antiques and antiquation, she hibernated until summer, never visiting her friends in their warmer houses; the hazards of getting about in winter were more than she could cope with, her purse not permitting a taxi or the proper clothes.

She saved her strength and her pennies for her summers in the Oval, where her social life centered on seeing old friends and the changes a year had made in their children.

The Oval contained the whole of her world. She had never accepted an invitation from any house outside it.

Her remaining days were too few to waste on the Johnny-come-latelies, whose antecedents were suspect, whose flaunted possessions were not always acquired by honorable means. Every year Addie wondered if she would live out the calendar the coal man gave her for Christmas. Her parents having left this life before they were fifty, Addie knew she had been born with their disposition to die. The whole Oval knew that Addie's inherited bad heart had always ticked on borrowed time. She was their invalid. They treated her tenderly, as if each summer were her last. And every summer that Addie was spared was a sign that God had some purpose in mind. In time it became an Oval legend that God was sparing her to attend Liz's wedding.

When Liz eloped to Greenwich weeks ahead of her scheduled wedding, with Addie's new dress already in her suitcase for its journey to the island, and a note in her strongbox advising her mourners that this was the dress for her laying out, her conscience thus eased and her pocket appeased, the Oval considered it a major miracle that Addie's bad heart survived the shock.

Corinne could do no less than offer Shelby as substitute whenever Shelby stopped dragging her feet and made her choice from the many acceptable men who would marry her in a minute.

The Oval was divided in sentiment, the solvent regretting their lost chance to glitter at a wedding in New York, the rest relieved that simplicity was the charm of a country celebration.

Though money was as important in the Oval as in any other upper-class community, it was not the determining factor in distinguishing between majors and minors. The distinction was so subtle, the gradations so fine drawn, that only an Ovalite knew on which level he belonged, and an outsider sometimes wasted an entire summer licking the wrong boot.

Occasionally, over recent years, an Ovalite flush enough to vacation abroad, or not flush enough to vacation anywhere, had rented his cottage to a family with the right credentials, who valiantly lived up to all expectations. This standard the Oval had set for itself was strictly adhered to until, of all ill-timed defaults, the summer of the wedding, when every cottage but Addie Bannister's was part of the preparations.

That Addie, a major Ovalite, should be the transgressor, Addie, whose impoverished heart had laid the groundwork for the wedding, that she had let down the class bars and unlocked her door to someone nobody knew but everybody knew about, was so plainly a symptom of her sickness that she had to be forgiven because, after years of false alarms, she was finally dying.

This time there was no doubt even in those doubting minds that had never entirely believed in Addie's bad heart. The few Bostonians who had seen her through the winter said that Addie looked awful, thin as paper and weak as water. They were not surprised that she had rented her cottage. Indeed it was a blessed relief not to have Addie sick on their hands when all hands were needed to help with the wedding.

All the same, Addie had betrayed her own code, which

counted money as the least of social accomplishments. With all the lovely people, friends of her closest friends, who would have been glad to rent her cottage the summer of the wedding, she had sold out to the highest bidder, someone to whom no one else would have rented a cottage for a million dollars.

But no one else was in Addie's shoes. She was mired in debt to her doctor and druggist for needles and pills that tried and failed, and to her patient grocer for the food on his shelves that failed too. These were debts of honor she could not bear to leave behind unpaid. And there was her funeral, likely come fall, with her small insurance not enough to cover it, and God knew she did not want to lie disgraced in a coffin for which some well-meaning meddler had passed the hat among his friends.

Her only salvation had been to rent her cottage, accepting the first extravagant offer, not caring, too frightened to care, whose signature was on the check, so long as the bank would honor it.

CHAPTER TWO

*T*he signature was Lute McNeil's, written in a bold, semi-literate hand. Yet that hand had a graceful elegance with the tools of his trade. Lute McNeil was growing rich in Boston as a furniture maker. The demand exceeded his supply. He was buying the four-story building in which he had once rented loft space, in which, before that, he had slept in the basement.

Success in business had not been Lute's boyhood dream. He had gone to vocational school and learned a trade mainly because he was an incorrigible who had been kicked out of secondary school. From his roaring mid-teens, succcess with women had been his only compulsion. Until the summer of the wedding he felt he had achieved it. Until the summer of the wedding, his values had never crystallized.

Lute McNeil, with his household of little girls, all of them by white mothers, none of them by the same white mother, with his succession of housekeepers, who sometimes were no more than that, and sometimes were much more than that, with his current wife, Della, refusing his demand for a quick divorce, and he threatening to expose their secret marriage to her Beacon Hill family—with all these complications in his life, Lute McNeil, the outsider, who had never set foot inside the Coles cottage, who did not even have an invitation to the wedding, was determined to stop that wedding because the woman he wanted was Shelby.

In the Addie Bannister cottage a screen door opened and banged shut. A honey-colored cocker spaniel, fat and elderly, waddled across the porch, took several sniffs of the morning, and settled down to survey it. In a moment the screen door opened and banged shut again as three little barefooted honey-colored girls, in T-shirts and shorts, the eldest carrying brush and comb, filed out and joined the honey-colored dog on the top step, the four of them solemnly and serenely waiting for Lute to begin their day.

Lute appeared on the porch, bursting through the door as if no door were there. The dog and the children swiveled their heads as one and looked up at him, the dog's tail thumping against the wood porch. From their Lilliputian perspective Lute stood giant size astride the world he had made for them.

He was tall, clean-limbed in his T-shirt and shorts, lean, lithe, nut-brown, with firm, well-cut features, dark, deep-set eyes that could hold and disturb, and close-cropped hair, wiry and strong.

McNeil was a borrowed name, borrowed by his mother from the man who was his father, or who she supposed was his father. For she was rough and ready, and nothing surprised her more than getting knocked up with a baby. She named him Luther after her father, who had thrown her out of his house for her wantonness, which made her rather proud of him for his stern stand on righteousness. She farmed her baby out to friends, who farmed him out to friends of theirs, until finally he ended up a state ward, his mother's whereabouts unknown.

Lute gave the dog a gentle nudge with his sandaled foot. "Go on, Jezebel, and take care of your business. You wouldn't move from dawn to dusk if somebody didn't make you."

Jezebel, who really did have business to take care of, got up and slowly descended the steps, giving Lute a downtrodden look, awash with insincerity. She dragtailed down the road in search of some suitable underbrush where her traces could be hidden, looking back once, her look again filled with wretchedness.

The group on the porch pretended not to see, and, as expected, Jezebel's tail abandoned its droop. Her nose made delighted forays in a zigzag course across the park, where the rabbits had romped under last night's moon, and her waddle increased to a fairly respectable trot as she abandoned herself to her joy in the morning.

With a swooping motion Lute caught his oldest daughter around her middle, sat down in her vacated place, and settled her between his knees. She handed up the comb and brush, and Lute set to with careful strokes to free Barby's hair from its tangled sleep.

It was long, lovely hair, paler gold than her sunburned skin. With her wide green eyes and delicate features, Barby was an enchanting eight-year-old, though no more appealing than her sisters.

Seated on either side of Lute, six-year-old Tina and three-year-old Muffin—her own corruption of her given name, Maria—waiting their turn to be brushed and braided, were like children from a painter's easel. Tina's hair was golden brown, shot through with silvery strands. Her long-lashed eyes were gray-blue. Muffin had chestnut hair that looked like burnished bronze after a brushing. Her round, inquiring eyes were dark violet.

"Daddy," said Barby contentedly, "you brush better than anybody."

"Daddy," echoed Muffin, "you brush better than anybody."

Lute was working expertly, smoothing out the waves, brushing away from Barby's face whatever stray locks were forming curls on her forehead.

"That's just because I've done it longer than anybody," Lute said. "But mothers are the best. You'd be surprised how good mothers are at everything."

"Isn't GiGi our mother?" asked Muffin, who had no idea what a mother really was.

"Of course not," Barby said with a weary sigh for Muffin's ignorance. "She's our housekeeper." And Mrs. Jones really was just that, Lute having got rid of the one who was something more soon after seeing Shelby.

"She's our housekeeper," Muffin repeated agreeably, though she still didn't know the difference.

"Did I ever have a mother?" asked Tina shyly. She was terribly afraid it was a stupid question, that she ought to know the answer. But it had puzzled her all summer to hear the children in the Oval talk about their mothers as if they had always had them.

Lute was plaiting Barby's hair now, weaving it into two tight braids. If before the day's end her hair, or her sisters', cascaded free, adding allurement to the beauty of their faces, at least Lute was trying to teach them modesty.

"All of you had mothers," he said to Tina, making his voice very matter-of-fact.

"Where are they?" asked Muffin in surprise, involuntarily looking around, half expecting they must be somewhere.

"They're divorced," said Barby calmly, not knowing that was a sad thing for a child to say.

"They're divorced," said Muffin happily, pleased that she had learned a new word.

"What does that mean?" Tina demanded. She did not want it to mean that they were dead, just when she was finding out that anybody could have one.

"That means Daddy wanted us and they didn't," said Barby, not minding.

Lute tweaked Barby's braids, the signal that he was through with her and ready for Tina. She and Tina shifted places, crawling over Lute like puppies.

He settled Tina between his knees. Reflectively he rubbed the back of the hairbrush along his nose, trying to figure out how to explain.

"It doesn't mean they didn't want you, mothers always want their babies. It means that when a mother and father get a divorce they can't divide the baby, so they have to draw straws. I was always lucky enough to draw the long straw."

"How many divorces did we have?" asked Tina, not sure she approved of them.

"Well, going on three," Lute said, trying to make them sound like perfectly normal happenings.

"Three," said Tina wonderingly. "Three divorces and three mothers." Next door there were three children and only one mother for all of them. Somehow she liked that arrangement. She knew that she would have hated it if she and Barby and Muffin had had three fathers. It was better to have just one of each. Except that they didn't have even one mother, for all that once there had been three. She wondered if Barby wanted a mother. Muffin never wanted anything but dolls so that she could boss them the way the housekeepers bossed her. But if Barby wanted a mother, maybe Daddy would do something about it. Daddy always said Barby had the most sense.

But Barby would never want a mother. She knew about mothers. They cried. She could not remember the face of her mother, but vividly, chillingly, she remembered the sound of her sobbing and, after her, Tina's mother's wilder sobbing, and now the one Daddy called Della, who was probably Muffin's mother, because in the night she sobbed too.

She said bluntly, before Tina could even ask, "I don't

like mothers. They make me nervous. They cry too much. They get mad too much, they call Daddy 'nigger.' "

It was a harsh word, an ugly word, a word that no one had ever heard her say. But she had to say it for Tina's sake. She could trust Muffin not to want a mother. But she was beginning to be doubtful of Tina, who was seeing too much of next door's mother. Tina didn't know what mothers were like when they were crying mad. She had been too little to remember—just as Barby had been too little to understand.

Lute said carefully, "Sometimes mothers say things when they're mad that they're sorry for when they're not mad."

But the children were not comforted. Muffin had clutched his arm while Barby was speaking, and Tina, even inside the nest of Lute's knees, moved uneasily. They were frightened by the forbidden word. Barby had heard their mothers say it. No wonder Barby didn't like mothers. Muffin screwed up her face in utter rejection of this species of woman. Tina tried hard to but somehow couldn't. The image of next door's mother intruded.

Next door's mother never cried. Whenever she looked at Tina, she smiled. Whenever she spoke, she said words that were loving. Every day she gave Tina a hug and a kiss, sometimes more than one, sometimes more than two. Tina had spent the shining summer in breathless expectancy of this ritual.

The children next door were only oblique excuses for going over to visit. Barby was scornful of them because they were boys who pulled her braids. Muffin beat them with her fists when they dangled her dolls out of reach and made her

15

say please. But Tina pretended that boys were fun to play with, although she was terrified if they played rough.

The way to heaven was not always easy, but getting there was worth the bumps and bruises. For next door's mother came to comfort. She was soft and round. To lean against her felt so different from Daddy. It felt safe, as if she could sink so deep into that warm and breathing softness that she would be hidden forever from everything that frightened her.

Next door's mother said Tina was the little girl she had always wanted until she gave up trying. It was plain that boys were not what she wanted. When she hugged them, they giggled silly and wriggled away. Tina didn't. She stood very still, mute and malleable. Time after time Tina got an extra hug from the love left begging by the boys.

Next door's mother had found Tina after she stopped trying. It was funny how things happened. It was wonderful how things happened. There never was a summer that had kept so many promises.

CHAPTER THREE

*M*uffin suddenly burst out laughing. "Look at Jezebel," she squealed, doubling over with delight.

They looked at Jezebel. She was picking her way across the park, walking slowly and sedately, with a large, unwieldy pancake suspended from her mouth. Presently she stopped, lifted one paw, and scanned the park for spies. Then she carefully put the pancake down and dug a hole beside it.

It was her morning custom to make the round of the cottages. As the only female dog in the Oval, she could walk across lawns and scratch on screen doors without fear of being chased by the males whose province she was invading. That she was old and spayed and oblivious to their overtures did not lessen their appreciation of her presence among them. She was a diversion from their daily squabbles, and her favors, such as they were, were impartial.

Jezebel took everything that was offered her and buried everything that wasn't a bone. What pleased her palate she ate on the premises. The rest she carried to the park. That she accepted, even begged for, what she did not want was greed. That she saved room in her stomach for what she did want was good planning.

The Coles place was her favorite and final stop. Having lost their old dog the winter before, the Coleses were partial to Jezebel. They did not give her table scraps; they gave her solid chunks of meat. Even in her own home Jezebel did not have it that good. A dog who has to live with children has to have a lot of messy leftovers mixed in with her daily rations.

Jezebel, her task completed and the earth packed back as neatly as if it had never been disturbed, now made straight tracks for the Coles place, panting in her lumbering haste.

Lute had bound Tina's hair into braids. He tugged at them, and her face bent back to him, its innocence dream-washed with love for next door's mother, even Jezebel's antics not wholly erasing it.

Impaling the love on that lifted face, Lute kissed Tina so hard that her teeth caught in the flesh of her lip, and a little trickle of blood filled her throat with nausea. As she clambered over Lute's knee to give her place to Muffin, he caught her in a bear hug that took her breath away. She gasped from the pain of it. Her ribs felt crushed.

"That hurts, Daddy," she said on a sob.

Barby turned beet red. "Stop it, Daddy," she said

fiercely, while Muffin beat on his arm, her hand being quicker than her tongue.

"You know I wouldn't hurt Tina," he said, trapping Muffin's fist and lifting her high above his head to make her laugh. "Tina knows how much I love her."

But no one knew really. It was immeasurable. Every man has a child that is his heart's child. For Lute it was Tina, born of his second wife, a Polack waitress, fresh from her chastity on an upcountry farm, her eye compelled to Lute's dark handsomeness in the row of amorphous white faces across the counter of a cheap beanery.

Lute made love to her in the loft. No trick to get her there, who had nowhere to go in the big, indifferent city, and no time wasted in seducing her, since he was a master at seduction and she a trembling novice, learning more than she could bear knowing, loving Lute and hating herself.

He married her, not because he owed it to her, but to give legitimate paternity to his child that she was carrying. For all the useful obscenities at his disposal he was never known to call anybody "bastard." And this Polack girl, to whom he had never shown tenderness, or been faithful to, or even acknowledged as his wife, once he had the paper to prove it, treating her like a servant, not even knowing how to treat a servant decently, mocking her Polack ways, never saying two words to her that did not have their roots in obscenity, this girl had called him "nigger, nigger, nigger" in a last-ditch stand against his deadlier venom, and given him the divorce he had been demanding ever since his infidelities narrowed down to one obsession, Della, cool and bored and

Beacon Hill, as far removed from his mode of living as the remotest star.

He reached up for Della and pulled her down, down to the level of his debauchery, and he wanted his divorce so he could marry her, whose consent to be married he had miraculously achieved, whose child, his child, without miracles, was already conceived.

Why Della, having tried marriage once and found it wanting, found it, too, an expensive entanglement that cost her a good deal of money to buy herself custody of her son, why she would jeopardize that custody, and the happiness and psyche of the son she adored, never knowing when he would know, knowing she could not face his knowing, why, with nothing to gain and all to lose, she would let herself go so far with Lute that there was nothing ahead but disaster was because she, like the Polack, whom she was so unlike, and the wife before the Polack, whom she was even more unlike, carried within her the seed of self-destruction.

That first wife had been walking the beat, waiting for Lute, or someone like him, to pass. She was a truant from junior high, a baby-faced tramp, hot in her pants, pretty as a picture. Any boy in school would have dated her, but that quirk in her preferred bad to good, black to white. She was a Miss Know-it-all who knew no more than she had read in dirty books.

She thought her rendezvous in the loft, toward which her quick, unhesitating step carried her down the night-emptied, echoing streets, past the night-mysterious buildings, her eye darting toward doorways, not in fear but for the thrill of the unknowable, and the sound of her squeaking shoes as lost and lonely as crying children—she thought these ecstatic nights, and the liquor she drank like water, and the pawnshop presents Lute bought her, made her a bold adventuress, beginning a life of love and luxury which would end on the other side of the ocean in the gilded palace and golden bed of a turbaned prince.

But she did not count the days, for the nights alone possessed her senses. And when there was no check mark to make on the calendar, she did not know how to tell Lute she had failed him as a mistress. She never told him. He saw her swelling breasts; he heard her slower step on the attic stairs, and the moaning in her love that was more protest than pleasure.

He married her and put her in a flat in a section of the city where poor black trash and poor white trash mingled indifferently.

He was not completely sure her child was his, but he wanted no child that was his to be born a bastard, and he took the chance, coldly preparing, though he had no plan, to kill both mother and child if the child showed no trace of being colored.

And the girl, no more wanting to be married than Lute because marriage was an act of morality, repeated the vows of chastity and obedience out of hatred for her misshapen body that made her think that since she was ruined for love forever it did not matter if she wore a wedding ring and pushed a baby buggy.

When her child was born, she could not forgive it for

staying alive. When her body heated and her blood ran hot again, she could not bear the baby's helplessness that bound her to its needs.

Lute tried to beat her into wanting her baby, and her outcries were love cries that goaded him into greater brutishness. He never saw her fondle the child, or talk to it, or respond to its needs without sullenness.

When he came home, he examined the baby, felt her stomach to see if it was full, felt her diaper to see if it was dry, buried his nose somewhere in her middle for the smell of her, clean or foul. And however it was with the child, howling in hunger or cooing in content, his hand left a welt on his wife, and he scorned her in the night, wanting no woman who did not want children, who made him remember that he had no memories of mother love.

They lived in their hell for three years, she taking whatever spillover of sex she could get from whatever delivery man came to her door and had inclination and time for it, Lute keeping no count, losing count, of the women he laid in the loft, women from the street on whom he practiced a savage carnality as if each wore the face of his mother, that face of which he did not know one line.

The day that he found his child alone—not that she had never been left alone, but that he had never found her alone, the child being so used to it that she had never prattled over it—he snatched her up and took her to a neighbor's, someone he knew by sight and thought an ugly, big, fat, greasy sight, but likely enough to be a stay-at-home, and have no man but the man she was married to, an ugly, colored woman he could trust with his child, while he went home to kill his white wife.

He went home and waited, and in the hours of waiting, with only his hands to kill with, and those hands not really made for killing, he decided it was sweeter revenge to kick the mother bitch out to sell what was worth nothing to him, to starve when it was worth nothing to anyone, and to die slowly and lingeringly, unknown and unwept in the way he hoped God had punished his mother.

She died without disease or drawn-out suffering or hunger in a back alley in Chinatown, looking like a lost child who would lie down anywhere to sleep or, if not found, to die. She had a room to go to, and a Chinaman waiting with love in his loins, but she had been too drunk to get from one bed to another, and too beset by fate to escape her destiny.

Lute buried her, because it was easy for the police to retrace her history from yellow man to black. The big, fat, ugly woman knew a widow woman, as plug-ugly and no-nonsense as herself, who became the first of Lute's house-keepers before he realized that a housekeeper did not have to be repulsive and could be good in bed for no additional money.

Between the loft and the housekeeper's bed there was no lack in Lute that made him desire the awkward innocence of the Polack, who never excited or satisfied him, unless there was in him some deep-rooted compulsion to father children who knew their father.

Now there was Muffin's mother, Della, wife number three, secret wife number three, and God knows, secret and still astounded mother, who had bought a piece of Lute's furniture, and then bought Lute by opening the doors of her friends to him.

He had waited outside those doors, hitching his shoulders, while a servant went to see if he was expected to use the front entrance. When that servant returned, Lute followed him into a morning room, where often Della had preceded him, deliberately, to enjoy his discomfiture at finding her there among her friends, who were not his friends, and never would be, talking past him, around him, and certainly over him, treating him as if he were part of his own furniture, her eyes never meeting his in communication.

The Polack felt the senseless blows he did not dare inflict on Della, stomached the swilling over of his frustration, and when she could bear no more, when to crawl back on her hands and knees to her own kind and kin and live with their scorn forever was better than being devoured alive, she gave Lute the divorce he had beaten out of her, and the child he had never let be hers, clutching to her uncomforted heart the worthless knowledge that his triumphs were too hard won to bring him any happiness.

Lute, loving best the gentle child of that gentle girl he had never even tried to love, his blood made water by Tina's tears, whose mother's tears had turned his blood to ice, was determined that Tina should have the best he could give her, whatever the cost to himself or anyone else.

In this small rented house of Addie Bannister's that could fit twice inside Lute's big house in Boston, where every stick of furniture was of his own design, while Addie Bannister's beds and chairs were, like their owner, on their last legs, Tina had been happier than Lute had ever seen her.

She loved the maternal eye of the Oval, where all the children were partly owned by all the watchful mothers, not knowing she played in the park on sufferance, or that her summer was almost over.

For Lute, Tina's summers in the Oval had just begun. No one would take away her joy in belonging. He had tried to fight for it clean. Now he would fight for it dirty. When the battle lines were drawn, he would have settled for a seat at the wedding, asking no more than this guarantee of his right to return to the Oval. But the Coleses had thought too much of a lousy invitation to write his name across it. They had forced the fight. Now he would settle for no less than the best they had to offer.

The gossip tossed back and forth on the beach buried Addie Bannister before the first snow. Yet with all his cash, and all his credit, he couldn't buy her dollhouse for Tina. The God-almighty Coleses would see to that with a quiet word to the bluenose Boston lawyer who handled her meager affairs.

Well, he didn't want this dollhouse. They knew what they could do with it. Next summer, and every summer until hell caught up with him, he would pull off his pants in the Goddamn cottage of the Coleses and sleep in the bed of their prize daughter.

Shelby was ripe for the reaching. He knew the signs of surrender. What did a white man have for her that he didn't have a hundred times over? He needed no more than an hour alone with her to break the crystal he could see through so clearly. There wasn't a woman he couldn't bring to her knees, begging for more, denying him nothing, not even her hand in marriage.

His children would dance at his wedding a whole lot sooner than these Ovalites would dance at the wedding they had printed tickets for.

He turned his look of triumph on Tina. "Who wants to come back here next summer?" he crowed, laughter crinkling his eyes at the expected answer.

"I do, I do, I do," all the little girls sang, their behinds bumping up and down in their eagerness.

Lute creased his brows. "But suppose we can't rent this house again? Suppose we can't rent a house at all?"

"Oh, what will we do?" they cried passionately.

"Let me think," Lute teased them. He thought profoundly, the little girls staring at him and hardly breathing. After a long moment his face brightened. He nodded in satisfaction, swiveled Muffin's head from front to back, and began to braid her shining hair. It was still too short to stay in braids much longer than it took to make them, but her feelings would have been outraged if he had not gone through the motions.

"There's a house here, a beautiful house, and a beautiful lady who lives in that house. She has pretty manners and pretty ways. She could teach you a lot. If I married her, we could live in her beautiful house every summer. She would take care of you and be your new mother. Little girls need mothers to help them grow up."

"Not me," said Barby flatly. "They want to do the boss-ing." All summer the Oval mothers had bossed their kids around and whatever kids came to play with them.

"Not me neither," said Muffin. "I'd rather have a new doll!" She wore out most of her dolls beating them up when they were bad.

"Let's try one," Tina pleaded. "Please, Barby, please. If she's too bossy, we can divorce her."

Barby looked at her sister. Tina was ready to cry, and she did not want Daddy to see Tina cry. The crybaby mothers had made Daddy hit them.

"Okay, okay," she said hastily, with Muffin disdaining to concur. "Who is she, Daddy?" she asked politely. In her heart she knew it didn't matter. Women were all the same, even when they were housekeepers. Sooner or later they cried, and Daddy hit them.

"That's going to be my big surprise," Lute said. "You wait and see. You won't have to wait long."

Tina looked at him searchingly. "Do you promise, cross your heart?"

Lute's voice was rough with tenderness. "I promise, cross my heart."

Tina squeezed her eyes shut and said a little prayer behind them. Please, gentle Jesus, let her be next door's mother. Let me stay in the Oval my whole life forever. Amen.

CHAPTER FOUR

*F*rom an upstairs window in the Coles house, old Gram, maternal great-grandmother of Shelby, peered down on the Oval at the dark man and his golden dark daughters, muttering her displeasure at all that had come to pass in the ninety-eight years of her trouble on this earth.

Once every neighbor had been white, and Gram herself as true white as they were, as all Gram's kin had been since the South's beginning, until Gram's own daughter, Josephine, crossed her true white blood, her blue blood, with colored, and broke Gram's heart.

Josephine was dead now, long dead, her defection forgotten by everybody but Gram. And here was Gram, left over from before the war, still unreconciled to the outcome of the war, with nobody in the Oval caring, and most of them not even knowing that her father had been Colonel Lance Shelby, with a huge plantation that took up half a county, a mansion that must have had fifty rooms, and slaves enough to make a small army, every one of them willing to lay down his life for Marse Lance, and accepting freedom only because it was forced on them.

And Gram, the born aristocrat, lived surrounded by descendants of slaves, with nowhere to die but among them, no grave to claim her but the one they put her in, and nothing to mark her bones from theirs on Judgment Day when heaven rolled back to receive those born to sit or serve at God's table.

The dream Gram dreamed was to lie beside her forebears, in the white-only graveyard of her kith and kin, far from the cruel North with its stubborn earth that would not open on a winter's day, casting aside the dead indignant body for a softer day, making death indecent, postponing its appointed hour with the dust from which it came, to which it was entitled to return.

There was so little Gram asked of life, just a way to go home to die. There was so little life had let her hold on to except sorrow. The only thing she had salvaged from the blessings that were hers at birth was the Shelby blood that pumped so slow, so thin a stream through her veins that now it gave no comfort to her weary heart.

She had been awake since dawn, snatched out of sleep by the smell of death on the sighing wind coming through the window, that smell like no other, a smell so faint that only the knowing know it, and too unmistakable to be mistaken. No way to describe it, no earthly way. Only imagery could give some kind of sense to it: it was like white carnations torn from their growing to wither and die in a dead embrace.

Gram had got out of bed and knelt beside it to pray. She had not been down on her knees in years, the way there and back being too long, too perilous. But she wanted to humble herself before God so that He would see that her faith surmounted her frailty.

Our Father, who art in heaven, Gram prayed with pious hands, there is death in the Oval. The spread of its wings will darken the sky and cast a shadow on the house intended. You know, as I do not, whose turn it is to enter into the glory of Thy kingdom. Don't let it be me. I am not ready. Once I was ready, and You did not see fit to take me. You sent me to live in a foreign land, You set me down in the midst of strangers and savages. I bore my burden, I never complained.

My back is bent with the burden of living colored. Lift it from me in my last days. Make my great-granddaughter Your instrument. She's marrying a man true white. Put it in her listening mind to live like white. Put it in her loving heart to carry me home to die. With all her life before her, she won't refuse her poor old Gram with all her life behind her.

I don't mean to meddle in the mystery of Your ways, O Lord, but they say Addie Bannister is doomed to die. If You want Addie Bannister, her house is down the road a way. I know the choice is Thine, not mine. But I wanted You to hear my side. Praise God for His goodness. Amen, amen.

Gram had got up off her knees, struggling up in obstinate sections, one hand clutching her cane, the other the bedpost, rising halfway, and a hand not holding, trying again, and a foot slipping sideways, another try and her cane caught fast in a fold of her gown, and Gram not knowing what was holding her down until she heard a ripping sound, then one major try with what strength was left to try, and this time Gram standing erect at last, her heart thumping hard, her head shaking a little, her eyes dark-ringed with exhaustion, and her sighs and groans half pain, half exasperation at a body too old to do anything easily.

And having risen, she tottered to her chair by the window to sit down and rest from it, her course well charted by things she could hold on to. For everything in Gram's room was firmly rooted to the floor, table and chair legs in rubber cups that resisted any pushing, the mats secured with metal tape that would not slide with a stumbling foot.

She wished she had her old rocking chair. She would like to rock herself back and forth, back and forth until sleep came to shorten the time of waiting for full day. But they had taken her rocking chair away because its motion might tip her or its rockers trip her. Oh, it was a hard thing to have a rag-doll body that the undiminished mind had such trouble to control.

The morning song of the birds began, not as sustained or full-throated or thrilling as their spring song, but still a summer canticle of runs and trills from a variety of participants, the chewink, the chickadee, the purple finch, the bobolink, the robin, and the blue jay, whose two flute notes in praise of the rising sun were in such contrast to his two harsh cries of warning when danger stalked the park. The mourning doves grieved in the tallest oaks, and their sad, droning utterance, repeated over and over, by its very monotony set Gram's head nodding in sleep.

She stirred at a peal of laughter coming from Lute's little girls. She blinked her eyes and saw Jezebel coming straight as a die, and knew what she was coming for, and what they would give her, a plateful of food, with enough solid meat on that plate to have put solid flesh on Josephine when enough to eat might have meant the difference between her holding on and her giving up.

That heartbreak daughter, Josephine, inheriting her father's frail spirit and the despair he had died of more than he had died of pneumonia, because he could not cope with the new society of rich white trash in which his kind had been dispossessed, Josephine could not cope with her hunger, too far removed in time and thinking from the great plantation Xanadu to be nourished by Gram's memories that were the elixir that kept Gram alive.

Josephine knew that marriage to a man who could feed her was her only escape from the terrible trap of genteel poverty. But there was no one to marry her. The few men she knew, had they proposed to her, had only their names to offer her, which were worth no more than hers as cash across a meat counter. The men with money were white trash, who had robbed the aristocrats of their sovereignty, and she would rather marry a colored man who knew he was dirt beneath her feet.

This choice between two evils was merely a figure of speech. Josephine was sure she would die an old maid with her bones sticking through her skin. Her prophecy came true prematurely. She almost died at seventeen of the stored-up hunger that raged inside her like a fire, consuming her senses, since there was nothing else to feed on.

Black Melisse, born at Xanadu, nursed with Gram at the same mammy's breast, heard that Miss Caroline's daughter, Miss Josephine, was bedded with fever. Melisse and Gram had played together as children, Melisse calling Gram "Ca'line" until she could handle a bigger mouthful, "Miss Ca'line," which she swallowed without difficulty or distaste, accepting it, along with Gram, as in accordance with God's master plan.

That they saw little of each other after their marriages was mostly because Melisse did not wish to intrude on Gram's poverty, which was no greater than her own but more hopeless because there was no hope for it.

Melisse cooked for the new rich, branching out into catering. She began to make money, and she saved it to send her son North to college when he was grown enough to go, wanting him out of the overturned South, where decent colored people took orders from white scum who, before the war, could not have set foot on Xanadu without being horse-whipped off it, with Melisse and Miss Caroline up in the tree house laughing fit to kill at those big splay feet kiting it back to the hills.

Melisse, looking at her fine big son, full of her good cooking, wished she could skim off some of his fat and put it on Miss Caroline's poor puny child, but she knew Miss Caroline would not appreciate this layer of black on white.

That son, Hannibal, was nineteen when Melisse sent him to Miss Caroline's back door with a great silver tray, covered with a snowy napkin cleaner than Gram could ever wash a napkin, with each fragrant dish containing food the like of which Gram had not tasted since Xanadu, and Josephine had never tasted at all.

Melisse had put the proper, respectful words in Hannibal's mouth, had coached him in humility. "Miss Ca'line, I'm Hannibal, ma'am, Melisse's boy. Mammy heard tell how Miss Josephine was poorly. She sent this tray to tempt her. Says it tastes a heap better than the mud pies y'all used to make in the good days. Says she knows your hands are full nursing Miss Josephine. Says she'd be proud to relieve you of cooking long as Miss Josephine needs you to wait on her."

He did not see Miss Josephine that day, and it never occurred to him to wonder what she looked like. She was quality, and if his mother chose to feed her because she was, he had no quarrel with her kindness, and not much interest in it either.

When Miss Josephine was strong enough for an outing, Melisse put Hannibal in a coachman's coat and hat, set him in the driver's seat of a hired rig, with a picnic basket beside him, and sent him round to take Miss Caroline and Miss Josephine for a ride in the country.

They drove out to Xanadu. Twice a week they took the same drive, for there was nowhere Gram wanted to go except back in time. Hannibal, with his back to the ladies, almost never seeing Miss Josephine face to face, let alone eye to eye, except when he helped her in and out of the carriage, or passed her things out of the picnic basket, like a waiter, never sitting, never eating until the ladies were through, Hannibal fell in love.

He really fell in love with the past. He, who could never have played any romantic part in it, fell in love with Gram's long-winded stories about Xanadu, which the Yankees had gutted before she was seven, so that her telling was an enlargement of everything.

Hannibal listened spellbound, but Miss Josephine, refusing to listen, thought about Hannibal going up North, and jealously wished she was going, too, anywhere, out of this dead dream that no telling could revive.

Gram should have been disturbed by Hannibal's inability to utter one coherent word in Miss Josephine's presence. The only thing Gram thought about Hannibal's thick tongue was that it was idiotic of Melisse to think more schooling would improve it. The Yankee scoundrels would take his money and cast him forth into the world with books only half understood in his head, and no skills at all in his hands.

But there was no one to train the Hannibals in the things they should know. Those who could have helped them to be what they were born to be could not afford their keep. In these changed times, what was to become of the Hannibals? Gone were the good masters, who cared for them like children all their lives.

Riding in the carriage supplied by Melisse, Gram felt concern for the future of Melisse's son. That their futures were entwined did not enter her mind; she would have had to be out of her mind for such a thought to flash across it.

It was years before such a thought crossed Hannibal's, years of separation from Miss Josephine and Miss Caroline, during which they both grew thin as paper. Gram, born rich, born an inheritor, had this proud knowledge to sustain her. Miss Josephine, born poor, born without expectation, had nothing but the hunger that was destroying her.

What kept her from going mad were Hannibal's letters to Melisse. Melisse came once a week to hear them read, bringing a treat—a pecan pie, a three-tiered cake. She had no excuse for bringing anything as nourishing as a bowl of stew, though the skin and bones of the ladies made her heart ache under its weight of fat. Nor did she know how to offer Miss Caroline money, though her handkerchief was heavy with it.

So Melisse sent the money in her handkerchief to Hannibal, smoothing it flat on her aproned lap, while Gram, disapproving of all that wasteful indulgence, wrote the letter that would enclose it. It was she who read Hannibal's letters to Melisse. Miss Josephine listened, though seeming not to, and envied Hannibal his Gulliver's travels, and thought about Hannibal, and thought more and more about Hannibal, there being no one else and nothing else to engage her mind.

When the heaviness around Melisse's heart choked her heart and killed her, the money under her mattress was tied up and sent to Hannibal, with Gram not even considering taking a penny to pay the postage that cost her more than she spent on stamps in a year.

After Hannibal's letter of acknowledgment, there was no more reason for him to write. He had not inquired for Miss Josephine, not knowing if it was seemly. He had not written anything on which Miss Josephine could dream. It was as if the end of Melisse was the end of everything.

Miss Josephine gave up, was in bed more than she was

out of it. No one knew what ailed her. The tiny annuity Gram had, from Papa's sole investment outside of the South, went into medicines that did not help. That check, two hundred dollars, that did not stretch and could not stretch, but had to stretch over twelve long months, was swallowed up in fretful sickness.

The prophecy renewed itself. There was only one thing in Miss Josephine's life: death by slow starvation, complicated by cancer of the soul.

CHAPTER FIVE

The day Melisse was laid to rest, Hannibal was taking his teacher's exam, praying he would pass it for his mother's sake, not knowing she was already dead for his sake, her drowned heart no longer pumping to keep up with the schedule of cooking and catering that had filled her old kerchief with paper money.

When Melisse lay dying, Gram sat by her side holding her hand, just as Papa had held so many dying colored hands, performing his last duty, his divine duty to those slaves who had served him long and faithfully.

Melisse, meeting death tranquilly because her work on earth, the education of her son, had been well done, did not want Hannibal to know that she was dying, or told that she was dead until the earth was over her, and wanted no midnight telegram knocking at his frightened door, but a letter, written gentle, saying that this was how she would have it, herself remembered alive, not dead, strong, not stricken, walking the earth, not under it.

Perhaps it was Melisse, the undying in her passed on to Hannibal, who guided his hand when he wrote his exam, though her own hand had never mastered a written word nor had her eye comprehended one. Yet she was born to be what she never got to be: a scholar. She loved the feel of books, the printed page, wanting knowledge for the sake of knowing.

When she was six and freedom day came, she jumped up and down on an old stump, laughing, and crying, and shouting, "I'se free, I'se free," then knelt by that stump to pray that Massa would let her go to learning school. But freedom left her without a master, and her mammy thought schooling was for white folks with soft hands. Melisse was taught to cook instead, and she did it well because she would have done well at anything.

When her son was born, she made up her mind that he would have white folks' schooling, and there was nothing else she pounded so relentlessly into Hannibal's head. And Hannibal, not knowing that this ambition was nonsense for one with his small talents, achieved the nearly impossible by dogged application.

When Hannibal arrived in New York and presented himself at the college of his choice, he was told, more in amazement than anger, that he had come more ill prepared for higher learning than any applicant in its history, and counseled to go back to high school, if he had ever been there.

He went to high school, by day and by night, through winter straight through summer. He never relaxed from his studies, advancing, not by leaps and bounds, but never falling back, and retaining everything once he had it fastened to his mind.

Finally he was ready for college, going to day classes, getting tutored at night, and waking at dawn to reach for a textbook. His major was history because Miss Caroline had sparked his interest in worlds that had already taken their place in time in contrast to the world of the present, which had not been tidied up in a book with an ending and an evaluation.

He was nowhere near top man in his class, but he was probably the most industrious. When he was handed his degree, no one was more deserving. Nor was anyone more thoroughly qualified for a teaching assignment in a secondary school, where the important thing was to promote his pupils.

In the San Juan Hill section of the city, Hannibal sat behind a big desk, with a roomful of boys subduing themselves to bear him out until the bell rang. He envied them their learning side of the room, and knew that, as much as there was inside his head, there was even more still outside it.

He went back to college for postgraduate courses, going nights now, working toward another ·degree, setting his sights on a professorship. And in that slow but adhesive way of his, he began to feel a biological urge, evolving from his step-by-step realization that a man does not work for himself alone or aspire for himself alone. The reward yields only half its worth. A life to be lived must be shared. A man is born sharing his life with his mother. When a man has no mother, he marries.

And because Hannibal had no mother to share his life or choose his wife, or snatch away the pen he picked up to write with, or feel his head to see if he had fever, or fling herself down before him and tell him he would do what he did over her dead body, Hannibal, acting on impulse for the first time in his life, sat down and wrote a love letter, half of it a letter of reference, stating his age, in case it was forgotten, his state of health, excellent, his occupation, his present salary, his chances of improving that salary, and the other half his solemn avowal of his unworthiness to woo so fair a lady, plus his fervent assertion that the whole of his life depended on her answer.

Taking that life in his hands, Hannibal addressed his letter to Miss Josephine, not knowing if Miss Caroline would send the whole South in a posse to lynch him, but convinced that he must mail his letter or die.

Miss Josephine received the letter on her twenty-seventh birthday, when she felt other than she would the day after, when there was no hiding herself from the fact that she was now officially an old maid, who must grasp at any straw so long as it kept the queerness from closing in.

She stood outside the post office, reading Hannibal's letter, dazed, white-faced, scarcely comprehending, but cling-ing, clinging to even this outrageous proposal because there was nothing else to cling to.

Miss Josephine went back into the post office, took the scratchy pen, wrote one blind line at the bottom of Hanni-bal's letter—"I guess so"—bought an envelope, addressed it, mailed it, and felt so faint she had to go home on the arm of a gentleman, who would have snatched his arm away had he known it was not the familiar hunger of their class that caused her giddiness.

On the way home the one thing she thought, not daring to think beyond it, was that, thank God, it was always she who fetched the mail, a child's proud prerogative, which she had not forgone, having no child to make her a mother, forced then to continue child to her own mother, and now a cunning child, keeping a secret.

There was one more letter from Hannibal, brief—for he was now afraid even a breath might blow the whole incredible, miraculous thing away—with money for the trip, and the extravagant promise that he would make her rich.

Josephine wrote a farewell note and pinned it to her pillow.

Dear Mama, forgive me. I am going North to marry Hannibal. I do not want to be an old maid, and no one but Hannibal has asked for my hand, no one else has money to feed me. I will never come back to shame you. From now on consider me dead.

And just as she was, not smartened up for the trip, look-ing nothing like a runaway bride, only looking as if she was going to keel over, with an empty suitcase purchased en route to the depot, Josephine boarded the train, and did keel over twice before she reached New York from the heat of the bridges burning behind her.

Gram, with her head held high, her eyes very steady, a smile firmly clamped to her lips, told her friends that Jose-phine had gone to take treatment from a doctor in New York who was famous for his cures. They knew she was lying—famous doctors were for those who could afford them —but they did not tell her so, which was all Gram asked of them. Let them think what they liked, that Josephine was locked in her room, turned alcoholic, turned mad. Whatever they thought, in their wildest thinking they would never think the worst.

Gram gave herself a few weeks to live at the longest. She wanted to die, even praying that the stabbing pains in her heart would release her from this insupportable life.

But as the months added up—months enough to make a baby—Gram was terrified lest she live to this crowning in-dignity. The pain in her heart increased but did not kill her. She waked on earth, not in heaven, to face a world which God had not made big enough for her and a mongrel grand-child to live in together.

Her imagination made the imagined child a monster. Though she had seen enough intermixture to know the per-centage of two-headed offspring was rare, intermarriage was something else, outside all her experience and, until Josephine, her credibility.

She knew, without need of prescience, that Josephine would never be so fortunate as to be childless. Having made her bed, she was bound to give birth in it. Unless—and here Gram's heart almost did stop—unless Josephine sought to destroy her child by destroying herself.

It was the baby, not Josephine, who almost took both their lives. Josephine, forgetting her advice to Gram to think of her as already dead, wrote piteously:

> *Dear Mama, I am dying. I have all I want to eat, and I cannot eat it. Hannibal is good and kind, and I cannot bear the sight of him. The doctor says I am homesick for you. I am six months with child, and I have no strength for it and it is taking what little I have for myself. I have made my bed, and now I must die in it. But I cannot die without knowing you forgive me. Please come to me.*

Gram put the letter down and began to cry, great wrenching tears welling up from deep inside her. The area of pain dislodged, and the frozen heart was freed to fill with yearning. The longing to see Josephine, who was her child, and was with child, and dying of it, was stronger than the shame of it.

Once more, her head again held high, Gram, inviting her coteria of decaying old friends to tea in cracked cups, told another big lie. Josephine's doctor had referred her to a specialist in Vienna. Whatever the cost, she had to go, and

Gram, of course, would go with her. God would just have to perform the miracle of the loaves and fishes. She could not say how long they would be away. If the climate abroad was more suitable to Josephine's condition, it would be folly not to stay.

Gram's friends wished her Godspeed and left her to pack. She wondered wryly if they thought she had murdered Josephine, buried the body, and was now in flight. But they would never report their suspicions to the police. They would never even discuss the case among themselves, knowing it was better to let well enough alone. The truth about Josephine would have knocked them down like ninepins. They, like herself, had too little left in their lives to have their faith in their divinity destroyed by Josephine's apostasy.

Within twenty-four hours Gram was on a train going North, she who had never surrendered to the North, uprooted at a time of life when the roots have grown too deep and spread too far for a spade to search them out. The impatient ax must finish the job, and the severing is like blood soaking into the earth. The whole is never whole again, for a whole is the sum of all its parts.

Gram took her place in Hannibal's house, sat at his table —with Hannibal standing—took charge of his child, exchanged civilities with his few acquaintances, and moved among the colored strangers, never one of them, but made part of them through Josephine's refusal to leave the sanctuary of her room.

Gram, who had hidden Josephine's dishonor from her own friends, now tried to hide Josephine's reversion from Hannibal's. She heard herself explaining to the well-meaning neighbors bringing gifts for the new baby that her daughter —she never referred to her as Josephine, unable to say it without its proper prefix and unwilling to offend by doing so —was making a very slow recovery and was not allowed any visitors. Whether or not they quite believed her was again unimportant as long as they did not know that Josephine, having come at last into full and shocked understanding of her calamity, could not endure the thought of them.

Gram kept up this lie, not for Josephine or Hannibal, who must have known no right could come from wrong, but for the infant child, Corinne, whom they had made together, though Josephine would not touch her, and Hannibal was afraid his big hands might crush her, a child with Shelby blood, Gram's grandchild, however tarred by Hannibal's colored sperm, but first of all, and above all, a helpless baby, neither black nor white in its need, that someone had to care for, that Gram, having felt its hungry mouth search her flat, dry breast, could not help but pity and, pitying, had to love.

Hannibal continued to call Gram Miss Caroline. But Gram no longer called him Hannibal, since, in the context of their relationship, it might have sounded like acceptance of him as a son-in-law. She called him Professor, Southern style, thanking God he had chosen teaching as his profession, but still bemused that it had come to pass.

Hannibal, hearing that courtesy title, was more determined than ever that one fine day Miss Caroline would say it because it was so. Gram became Hannibal's lodestar. As it had been when he was a boy driving her back in time to Xanadu, the old romantic images of her grandeur returned, recreating the aura in which she moved for him. She supplanted Josephine in his planning. He would not stop with a professorship. He would make his ultimate, unrelenting goal a college presidency. He knew the college he intended to head. A Negro college in Washington that had never had a Negro president, but would have one in him, according him, as was his due, a staff of servants to wait on Gram, as was her due.

In the meantime he waited on Gram himself. He did the cooking because he was the better cook, and because he was busy in the kitchen he spared her having to break bread with him. He carried Josephine's trays up to her and made a few polite remarks, which she ignored, with her face turned away. Josephine, who had made herself his equal in bed, from that same bed now acted like his better. And Hannibal, who had Miss Caroline to fulfill his ideal of an aristocrat, was quietly amused, and played out Josephine's fiction that he was only there to serve.

Hannibal got his doctorate and his appointment to a professorship at the college in Washington. The child, Corinne, was fair enough to look white, which was the special hallmark of the blue-vein society in which she was to grow up and acquire her prejudices.

The blue-vein society, so styled because all its members had sizable amounts of blue blood in their veins, injected in some past generation by some passing senator or such, overlooked Hannibal's unfortunate color because of his professorship, and because he never accepted purely social invitations anyway, and did not darken their functions.

It went without saying that Josephine could not be persuaded to grace them. With a servant in the house and a bell to summon her, Josephine made imperious use of that bell and the servile attitude and accent it commanded. She rang it almost constantly, and she rang for food. There was nothing else she could think of to ring for, nothing else that gave her such a feeling of blessed forgetfulness.

Every night she sent for Gram. She wanted to hear about Xanadu, closing her ears to any capsule of current happenings, demanding stories of the great plantation, and listening with shut eyes so that she would drift into dreams divorced from the here and the hell she had made Gram a part of, with Gram not really feeling much like talking about Xanadu after a long, busy day with her granddaughter.

Hannibal became head of his department, with a bigger house and another servant for Miss Caroline. He ate most of his meals off a tray in his office. At home a tray was brought to his den, where he made a show of pushing his papers aside to make room for it. Gram instructed the servants not to set a place at table for him unless they were told. Hannibal saw to it that they never were.

Hannibal did become the first Negro president of his college, and was the equal of his predecessors, because of his clock-round devotion to duty. Gram became the grandam of the faculty wives, having that title thrust on her as she had thrust the title of professor on Hannibal, but unlike Hannibal, with no desire to make it meaningful, yet forced, for Corinne's sake, to accept with grace the unsought flattery, while Josephine, who had started it all, stayed out of it all upstairs.

Josephine died at forty-five in the fullness of her flesh. Like Melisse, she died of her obesity. They were not even sisters under the skin. They were just two women, worlds apart, who ate as much as they could hold, and died when they could hold no more.

With Josephine handsomely laid to rest in a Negro cemetery, to Gram—standing whitely by, thinking God knows what heartbreaking thoughts—was left the bitter legacy of living colored, with no one now who was true white with whom she could identify herself, and herself not even able to make a mother's wish that she had died instead of her daughter, for Corinne, who knew no other mother but Gram, no other loving, no other comforting, would have been more bereft than Gram was if Gram's hand had been lifeless in her grasp.

And now Gram was ninety-eight, wanting a hand to cling to herself, wanting Shelby's hand because it was being joined in marriage with a true white one, and that union, in the time of generations, would return to its origination, the colored blood drained out, degree by degree, until none was left, either known or remembered.

Gram picked up her cane and started that long, long walk to Shelby's room, on her way back to living true white, her cane and her trembling old hand along the wall giving what little help they could.

CHAPTER SIX

$\mathcal{L}$iz came up the hall stairs, carrying Laurie. Fresh from bottle and bath, the baby was full of infant play, her body bouncing inside her blanket and her hands snatching like petty thieves at anything they could grasp—a button, a strand of hair, a patch of skin. Gurgles of good will spilled out of her busy mouth in little bubbles.

Liz was on her way to Shelby's room, where she took Laurie every morning, tucking her into bed with her sister so that the warmth of her baby girl's body would begin Shelby's day. If anyone asked, Liz left Laurie with Shelby to give herself an hour or so of time to herself before Corinne awoke and took the house in hand, but it was in fact a calculated act of love on her part, a tender ruse to reinforce the blood tie between her child and her sister, and infect them with the habit of each other. If anything—knock on wood—ever happened to Liz, she wanted Shelby to be Laurie's second mother. Not so very long ago that was the way it had been with their dolls. When one of them was sick enough to spend the day in bed, which scared her into thinking about dying, the other always solemnly promised to be second mother to the other dolls, to love them as much as she loved her own, to raise them as one family.

Laurie was certainly more precious per pound than a doll. If Linc remarried, Shelby would have to be Laurie's second mother, and that husband-hunting hot pants who bedded him could beat her own brats. And if Shelby's white husband didn't want a colored man's child around, he wouldn't have Shelby around long either. Her colored blood would choose between them. It better.

Liz left Laurie snuggled deep into the crook of Shelby's arms and tiptoed away to take the quick shower that would have to stand in for the lazy loll in the tub that her body cried out for. Between the innocent demands of that child and her mother's anxiety about every nuance of the wedding, she wondered if she'd live to see Labor Day. She did the baby's wash, wishing she didn't resent this messy part of being a mother, then sat down briefly for a cigarette and a quick gulp of coffee, the instant kind that instantly kills all desire for another cup.

It was not the breakfast she would have chosen, but at least the hot drink gave enough of a charge to wheel Laurie around the Oval an hour later, while the family ate their beautiful bacon without a crying baby for company. At home she ignored Laurie's cries unless they were howls of pain, but here everyone rushed to pick her up and pet her as soon as she let out a peep. Everyone but Gram, who didn't rush because she couldn't and wouldn't even if she could.

Liz parked the baby carriage by the kitchen door and scooped Laurie up in her arms. It was still early. She crept into the kitchen and up the side stairs. Nearing the top, she heard Gram tentatively striking the floor with her cane, feeling her way as if testing the hall for traps. Her slippered feet shuffled unsteadily forward with grim purpose. What in God's name was she doing out here alone at this hour, a woman who couldn't remember the last time she awoke before eleven? Was she going to be difficult in this last week before the wedding, when months of careful planning hung in the balance?

"Oh, Gram . . ." Liz murmured reproachfully. "What are you doing out here? Why didn't you ring if you wanted something? Just because everyone in this fool house has lost their mind with this wedding, nobody's going to forget about you. For Mother's sake, please stay put. Let me take you back to your room. I'll go wherever you were going and do whatever you want done."

"You can't," Gram said. "You've got that child."

"Gram," Liz said for the hundredth time that summer, "call her Laurie. You screw up your face every time you call her 'that child.' If it hurts you to be so mean to a baby, why bother?"

Gram thumped her cane. "Keep a civil tongue in your

head. You're not so grown that I've forgotten how many times I've changed your diapers. What you call mean I call blind. My sight's no younger than the rest of me—old eyes like mine have to screw up to see a dark child."

"Gram, you say 'dark' as if it were a dirty word. You're not that blind; you've just got a blind spot. Look at Laurie's skin beside mine. Hers makes mine look washed out. Maybe past generations had color prejudice, but my generation has color appreciation." Liz held the baby out to Gram, who shrank against the wall for support, for succor, as the tiny hand reached out to her.

"Touch her, Gram. You've never touched her. Something will happen when you do. It happened to me. I was never mad for a baby, I was just mad for Linc. I loathed the whole business of being a mother. I hated the heaviness that kept me from my husband. I hated my howls when Laurie was being born. I hated all that bloody mess for a girl, and having to do it all over again if Linc wanted a boy. Then they held Laurie down to me and I touched her. Just as you once touched my grandmother Josephine, and Mother, and Shelby, and me. That's when the miracle happens. The first time you feel the flesh of your flesh. Laurie's the flesh of your flesh to the fourth generation. Touch her, Gram. I promise a miracle."

But now Gram really could not see the child. She was made dizzy by the words coming out of Liz, the intimacies, the indignities. Flattened against the wall, she seemed without substance, as thin and crackly as paper, as if she had borrowed time from that baby and must now release it. "It's not her fault that you married her father. Why did you raise up Lincoln? Why didn't you let his darkness die with him? Josephine sowed and I reaped."

Her head sank forward from the weight of her impotence. Her tears were as dry as the dust her sorrows had stirred. She looked so old, so stricken, that Liz's spurt of hot anger shied away from its target and thrashed itself out in her stomach.

"Gram, stop it. Stop it. Stop it. You make me feel sick. No matter how white the rest of us are, we're just as colored as Laurie. It's your race that says so. Laurie's no different from me, just darker. The rest of your life would be so much easier if you'd only stop picking the scab off the sore."

Gram's head began to shake as if it were coming loose from her rigid body. Her voice was full of crying in the wilderness of time outlived. "Don't hammer at my head until it rolls at that child's feet. Don't choose this morning to destroy me. There's death in the Oval. I woke to the smell of it. That smell never fools me. Maybe, maybe it's me that's marked, but it doesn't have to be. It could as soon be that friend of your mother's—you know the one—who never comes into this house without complaining about her heart."

"Why would you wish the worst to Addie Bannister? She never came into this house without remembering to ask for you. She likes you. You're the only one whose background she doesn't pick apart. She's almost a member of the family: don't wish a wake on Mother along with Shelby's wedding."

"I wouldn't put bad mouth on Addie Bannister," Gram said shrilly. "I don't believe in bad mouth. All I'm saying is, death is here waiting for somebody. It's your mother who says it's Addie Bannister. It's your mother who says she's nothing but bones. It's your mother who says if she tries to come down her heart won't stand the excitement. And I will tell you this—if death is sparing me for some other hour, some other place, I want to go home to die. That's all I'm saying. I want to die at home. If you and your child will step aside, I'll go ask Shelby to take me."

But Liz took a protective step forward, partly to shield Gram from the specter of her own senility, partly to save Shelby's day from a depressing start. Gram would live forever; wasn't she doing it? "Gram, you don't want to go back to New York today. Shelby's getting married tomorrow. Both of you should be here. You wait and go home with Mother. Summer's almost over. Another two weeks and we'll all be packing up. Let me take you back to your room and ring for your breakfast. You had a bad dream. That's all that happened. A nice hot breakfast will help you forget it." She shifted the baby and took Gram's arm to turn her in the opposite direction.

Gram shook her arm free. Like a windup toy that has been wound up too often, she turned herself around with a painfully slow, jerky motion, her cane tapping angrily. With what breath she had she hissed fiercely, "Keep ahold of that child before you drop her and say 'twas me who made you. I'm going back to Xanadu, and you can't stop me."

Her journey aborted, her toilsome walk having led to nowhere but Liz's dark baby, Gram used her elbow to steady herself along the wall, so that her hand could hold her heart to keep the hope from running out of it.

CHAPTER SEVEN

$\mathscr{S}$helby awoke to the laughter of Lute's little girls too, their golden sounds penetrating the edge of her sleep and stirring her consciousness from its dream and into the waiting morning. She flung the covers back, wanting to be free of even this slight encumbrance of sheet and summer blanket. Leaning forward, with her knees drawn up to let the covers slide down them, she was in a cocoon of herself, the scent of her body, the clean smell, the warm smell, striking her nostrils sharply before it dispersed itself amid the breeze-borne scents of the onrushing day.

Jezebel barked in rapid-fire frustration—her squirrel bark. Some squirrel was no doubt far out of reach in the maple tree outside Shelby's window, teasing her, probably by flicking its tail. It was a tree that no fat dog could climb for all her foolish clawing at the trunk, but claw she did, as if her industry would bend the bough and pop the succulent squirrel into her mouth like an apple ripe for eating.

The barking stopped. Shelby knew that Jezebel was sitting on her stern at the front of the tree, her back bolt-straight, her neck stretched tight, her eyes unblinking and alert, her tail swishing back and forth as she tested her patience with the squirrels, not having learned from daily experience that she would give up first, her rheumatism rebelling against the strain on their summer truce, and her common sense advising her that a bone near at hand in a friendly house was more inclined to her persuasion than a treetop squirrel of unknown taste and toughness.

Shelby had had a puppy once, not a family pet with papers but a puppy of her own of infinite and interesting extraction. She was six when she acquired him, coming upon him deep in the berry-thick woods, where she was never supposed to go alone. But she had awakened one morning before anyone else, unable to wait another day for some forgetful grownup to take her to see if the berries were ripe. She fetched along her sand pail in case they were, and solemnly promised herself to stay within a stone's throw of the house.

The pedigreed family dog, looking at Shelby with one half-opened eye and listening with only half an ear, was not bestirred to action by her preparations. He knew what children did with sand pails. They made mud pies. He closed his eyes, folded his ears, and fell asleep, never dreaming that Shelby was going out to get lost, and never to live down the shame of letting her.

At the edge of the Coleses' back property Shelby

searched around for a stone, rejecting one after another in her search for one that would leave her inexpert hand with more speed than a large one.

She made a wild throw and marked the spot with her eye, which had no more accuracy than her aim. When she reached the spot, surprised and delighted that she had thrown so far, the bushes just a little beyond seemed to beckon her with their abundance. But even these could not compare with the bigger, bluer berries only one, only two, only three steps ahead, which somehow steadily shrank in size as more and more richly burdened bushes impelled her in every direction.

When she thought to look back, her house was gone. Its disappearance did not frighten her. A house was too big to get lost. She would find it exactly where she had left it, and nobody would scold her when she showed them the fruits of her disobedience.

Coming to a halt at last, she carefully selected a berry, licked it for taste, and dropped it into her pail. And as she listened to the round plop of its plumpness, she heard a stirring in the ground cover of leaves, the stubborn oak leaves of last fall, not yet decayed, not yet without sound nor yet turned into timelessness.

Shelby stared around her and saw two eyes staring back, two wistful brown eyes belonging to a dog with his head between his paws in the ancient attitude of submission. In her astonishment, Shelby let her pail fall from her hand to lie forever with the strange debris of the woods left behind by man in his eternal haste to get somewhere other than where he was. Slowly, and with hands outspread in the way she had been taught, Shelby approached the puppy, believing him hurt and unable to move, making soft little motherly sounds to comfort him.

Kneeling beside him, she saw he was not hurt but trapped, his lead caught fast in a tangle of briers. Seeing the lead, she surmised that he had jerked away from whatever hand had held it too loosely. He had probably seen or scented a rabbit, and followed its elusive trail to his own disaster.

Still murmuring gently, Shelby tried to dislodge the lead, but each time she pulled the puppy choked and whimpered, his neck already rubbed sore by his own frantic tugging. She knelt beside him again, her head against his, to reassure him that she was there to help not hurt him, as soon as she figured out how. In a second or so she did see how, and unfastened his collar.

Set free, the puppy rose and almost shook himself apart ridding himself of brush and kinks. Then he leaped on Shelby with grateful kisses. She fell without bruise or scratch and laughed at the suddenness of her descent. The puppy, taking her laughter as a signal to play, romped all over her, and for a while they roughhoused together, forgetful of everything except this outburst of energy.

When they quieted, both lay panting, snuggled against each other. Presently, they were both sound asleep.

When they awoke—the turning and twisting of one arousing the other, and hunger immediately besetting them both—the Coles household was already assembling for breakfast, with Liz being sent in search of her sister before Shelby committed the childish act of eating at some other table an Ovalite mother felt obliged to set for her.

But Liz, too, was long delayed, not by invitation but by children who had already eaten but wanted to stay and play. Nine-year-old Liz, taking at least one turn at whatever game was under way, let precious time pass before she turned to report on her missing sister.

By now more than a mile away, Shelby and the puppy, the lost and the found (for Shelby was now lost too even if she did not know it), started off in a southerly direction simply because that was the way they were facing.

"We're going home to your house," Shelby said commandingly. "Your family doesn't know where you are. You ran away and lost them. You'd better show me where they live or they will be mad at you."

The puppy bounded ahead and she skipped along behind him, the blind on the heels of the blind, neither with any notion which way either was going, and each believing the other had sense enough to go home.

Some time later they came out of the woods within sight of the boat-dotted sound. There were waterfront homes in front of them, and people on porches, but the puppy did not even glance in their direction and none of them rushed to claim him. Shelby stopped walking and the puppy did too, looking up at her inquiringly. "I guess we'd better ask somebody if they know you."

They turned up a flagstone walk bordered with sweet alyssum. At the foot of the porch, an elderly couple leaned forward in their rockers, the better to study them, in particular this lovely child, this picture-book child of six or seven or so with dark blue eyes and blond curly hair, wearing a yellow berry-stained sunsuit and bright red sandals beneath brier-scratched legs.

"Hello, little girl," the elderly woman said.

"I found a doggy," said Shelby without ceremony.

"Did you find him or did he find you?" the woman asked, knowing that children did not always recognize this distinction.

"I found him in the woods," said Shelby stoutly. "He was all tangled up in the bushes where I was picking berries."

"Well, I don't think he belongs around here," the gentleman said with a doubtful look at the puppy, who bore no resemblance to any of the pedigreed breeds found in the waterfront houses.

"But you live near here, don't you?" the lady asked Shelby, with another appraising stare that confirmed her first impression that Shelby was of the breed that belonged, and was probably a visiting cousin. Shelby answered that she did not live near, not wanting to confess that she had strayed farther than a stone's throw, and not knowing that the distance she had come was the infinite distance between two worlds and two concepts of color.

"Well, you'd better go home, dear, before your family misses you. Stay on the road and don't go back through the woods. It's a wonder you didn't get lost. And you mustn't fret about the dog—he'll follow you home and your family will know what to do with him. Run along now, straight home."

"I will," said Shelby, really glad to be given a command, which relieved her anxiety about the puppy and instructed her to go straight home, where, with her hunger and thirst nagging her now without letup, she wished she was this very minute.

Shelby and the puppy returned to the road and resumed their search for some familiar house or face. Many people saw them pass—most of them smiled, some even spoke a greeting, and all of them absorbed the beauty of the bright-haired child, even taking casual note of the yellow sunsuit and the red shoes. None of them suspected for a moment when they were later questioned that Shelby was the colored child who had now been missing for over four heartbreaking hours.

A sand pail had been found in the woods and identified as hers, and the unspoken fear was now growing, since no one anywhere had seen her, that she had gone through the woods to the waterfront, stopped to play in the water, waded out too far, and drowned. But the land search went on in the desperate hope that the child would be found alive and un-harmed, with no one yet willing to abandon that hope and drag the sea for a small drowned body.

The sickness of the search was that so many people saw Shelby, but they were not looking for such a child. They were looking for a colored child, which meant they were looking for what they knew to be a colored child—dark skin, dark hair, and Negroid features.

A snowballing word of mouth, a genuinely sympathetic mouth, had needlessly falsified the child's description by its thoughtless indulgence in that strange habit of whites of prefacing any and all mention of colored people with the identifying label of race.

For, as the alarm had spread through the town that a child from the Oval area had been lost, those who knew where the Oval was had added the helpful information that an Oval child was a colored child. Shelby had made the subtle transformation to a little colored girl wearing yellow and red, which made the stereotype complete.

Even the police and the organized volunteers hampered their own painstaking search by coloring their inquiries. For even they did not believe they were searching for a blond-haired, blue-eyed child, just as the two old people on the porch had nothing in their experience to imagine such a phenomenon. Those who knew colored people only as servants and veered from thinking of them otherwise could not make any association between the poised and lovely child who had brightened their morning and the colored child who had gone and gotten herself lost.

Even the yellow dress and the red sandals did not strike them as anything more than an unremarkable coincidence. Every little girl had a pair of red shoes. Red was childhood's favorite color. And yellow was becoming to blondes. In envisioning these unsuitable colors on a colored child, they evoked no image that could possibly compare with their recollection of Shelby. They said they had not seen her, and watched the searchers go off. In a way, they were better off not knowing how unhelpful they had been, and better off not knowing that they had glimpsed in Shelby the overlapping worlds and juxtaposed mores they would not live to see.

It struck the old gentleman that he should call after the

retreating form of the police officer and tell him that a dog was missing, too, but he thought better of it. They had enough on their minds without this bit of frivolous information.

So they slowly rocked in their chairs, staring at the incoming tide and praying that it held no cruel surprises. For although the interior life of a small colored girl was far beyond their ken, the love of parents for their children was not, and in their own way they hoped this child would emerge from the woods to fulfill her life's potential, however obscure it seemed to their old, pitying, prejudiced eyes.

Every passing hour pushed Corinne closer to the moment she most dreaded, the moment when she would have to telephone Clark in the city and tell him—the man who asked nothing more of her than that she take good care of his children—that somehow a child had gotten mislaid while she slept more soundly than a mother had a right to, and that all the police and all the town could not find her. She knew that Clark would clear his office of patients and sit behind the locked door waiting for her next call or for the next island-bound plane, whichever came first. His nurse would be beside him, Rachel, the other half of him, his wife without a ring. She would wait beside him as she was so used to waiting, childless who wanted children, faithful who did not have to be, patient who schooled herself in patience, knowing she was neither the first woman nor the last to love a married man who could not cut his wife and watch his children bleed.

Corinne's trembling hand tried to steady itself enough to reach the telephone. With more miles between herself and

Clark than any man-made miracle could bridge, she saw without need of second sight his stunned recoil from the torrent of her terror to the quiet waters of Rachel's calm reassurance.

In his agony of spirit, his blood and flesh would turn to her, going deep into the never dry well of her incredible brown body. He would go to her bed, to the flat that he paid for, not to possess her at such a cheap price, but to convince her that this was his home away from home much more than was the summer place where he spent the month of August missing her and taking his only delight in his children.

Corinne had the telephone in her hand, but her mouth had grown chalky and her tongue felt dry and swollen. The number would not form in her mind, for she had been suddenly overwhelmed by the thought that it would be Rachel who would answer the phone, Rachel who would with brittle formality say that Dr. Coles was out, did Mrs. Coles want to leave a message? She would have to tell Rachel her terrible story, and they, the haters, would have to speak to each other intimately. For they were both bound to the father of that lost child until the day came in some far future when Shelby was old enough to fall in love and free her father to marry the love of his own. But Corinne knew from past experience that Rachel's first wave of sympathy and concern would quickly abate, and that her next thought would be fueled by her resentment that in her ripe and willing womb no seed had ever been allowed to germinate, in keeping with Clark's code that no one of his blood would ever have a child they had to hide. She, who would have given Clark the ultimate manifestation of love, was forced to wash her children away, while Corinne—whose womb had been made safe for self-indulgence with the men who were dark enough to excite her—could never replace a lost child for a living one, or bear the son for Clark that lived its useless hour in Rachel's loins.

It was true that in the nighttime of love Corinne desired and was possessed by the very darkness that repelled her in the day. Her repulsion was grounded in a suspicion that, given her forebears, only chance had given her the proper, fair color. Chance had smiled again and given her two daughters in her likeness, but Hannibal's half of her makeup still had to be heard from, and the chance of that pattern continuing unbroken was too slight for her to risk a third try at bearing Clark a son. Her fear that she might reject her child as Josephine had rejected her was too deeply rooted in her psyche for her to drag it up to the surface and damn the consequences.

Suddenly her face went slack around her open mouth and she collapsed, the floor rising up crazily to slam her in the face. The local doctor came and she was put to bed under mild sedation. She slept fitfully, softly whimpering.

Gram, already past eighty at this point, took up the watch. She sat quietly on the enclosed porch, erect in a hard-backed chair. A pane of glass shut her out from any strength-draining conversations with the neighbors who silently stood vigil on the lawn, quieting the children when their voices shrilled, allowing Gram the dignity of her isolation.

In a summer settlement some distance from the Oval but very like it in its quiet location and little park, the mothers gossiping back and forth about the lost child and the waning hope of finding her alive felt great sympathy for the Negro mother. They wished that there were some way they could help, for they knew that it could have been one of their own children as well as not, and they thanked God for sparing them. From time to time they made a careful check of these children, screeching a little one's name whenever a panicky eye overlooked the object of its search. It was some time before anyone noticed that the protective circle of neighborhood children included one more child than it should, and one more dog. For a while the child was left to itself, each mother thinking rather smugly that *her* small child was where she could see it. This was no day to let children run free.

Shelby had been drawn to this sanctuary because it resembled home, with its little park and its children playing and its mothers watching them. She found a tree to stand under and leaned against it, thoroughly tired after the long walk through the heart of town. For the first time that day it occurred to her to be worried about her situation. The puppy was nervous too, as if he sensed her anxiety. He darted from beneath her feet and into the street and back again, over and over, several times narrowly avoiding a grisly fate beneath onrushing wheels. The summer cars honked at the puppy impatiently, until finally a policeman, terribly conscious that his summer job existed because of them, told Shelby a little too tartly that her dog was tying up traffic. "*Go* home and *tell* your mother that all dogs must be restrained on a leash downtown. Or their owners will be fined."

Shelby could only stare back. She was too overcome at

being the sudden center of attention, a dozen honking cars screeching to a standstill, and a tall policeman, as tall as the sky, crying sharp words that she couldn't unscramble. On top of it all, the puppy—not knowing a friend from an enemy—insisted on digging his paws into the policeman's impeccably creased pants as he begged for water, using the only sign language he knew.

Shelby, older and shyer than the dog, kept her own extreme exigency to herself, though it was rapidly reaching an excruciating state. Bracing herself against the tree, she clamped her legs together and began to shiver uncontrollably. She tried desperately to find a dark face among the crowd of mothers. She simply knew that a dark face was almost always an approachable face, while a white face was always a passerby's face, one of so many that it was impossible to pick out the right one. Her straits were too intimate to reveal to a stranger.

Suddenly it happened, before all these strangers, as the puppy sniffed at her and looked surprised, and a boy stopped dead in his play and stared before running off to tell. The hot sticky stream ran steadily down her leg, making little splashes around her feet. The children stampeded to witness her disgrace, their eyes crowding in, and then giggles rising around her like waves, like waves drowning her.

She cried and cried and cried. She turned her back and pressed her scarlet face against the tree.

Then there was a voice, a mother's voice, scolding but not scolding her, shooing the other children away, reminding them that they were not immune to accidents. The arms gently pulled her away from the tree and held her racing heart against a quiet hill, and a clean, soft handkerchief with a scent she could never know but never forget dried her downcast face. The voice, as gentle as snow falling, slowed her shuddering and her sobs.

"What's your name, darling?" the mother's face asked.

"Shelby."

There was something about that name that sounded familiar. "Shelby what, dear?" the woman asked.

"Shelby Coles."

That sounded even more familiar. The mother called to the watching women. "She says her name is Coles. Does that ring a bell?"

It did for somebody. "That sounds like the name of that colored child they're looking for. Seems to me it was Coles or something like that."

"So what?" someone else cried out. "It takes more than a name to change black to white."

"I'm not blind," the mother said indignantly. She turned back to Shelby. "Run home, dear, and tell your mother to change your clothes and keep you home so you don't get lost."

"I am lost," said Shelby softly, admitting it to herself for the first time, and unable now to go another step unless it was in the direction of home.

"This one's lost too," the mother groaned. "Are you sure you don't know the way home from here?"

Shelby nodded mutely.

"But at least this one's been found. I just hope her family isn't too frantic."

"The quickest thing to do is to call the police in case

they've had a call from her mother. Tell me your name again, dear, slowly."

"Shelby."

"Tell me your whole name."

"Shelby Coles."

This had to be more than a coincidence. Reason rejected the possibility that two children were lost with the same name and the same outfit. And yet it was just as improbable for a white child to be colored, but what else was there to think? She called to the women. "One of you come here for a moment. Just one. Too many might frighten her."

A woman quickly outran the others, sniffing something special and wanting to be part of it. "What's wrong?" she asked.

"I know you're going to think I'm crazy, but this has to be the child they've been looking for."

"You're crazy, all right. You really think so?"

"There's only one way to find out."

"How?"

"Ask her."

"Ask her?" The mother was horrified. "I couldn't do anything so awful. Suppose she isn't? It might leave a scar."

"Well, we're wasting time this way."

The mother looked at Shelby carefully, studying her blond, sun-bleached tresses and her beautiful blue eyes. "It's a fool question, but I'll ask it." She took Shelby's hand. "Tell me, little girl, and don't be afraid. Are you colored?" Without knowing it, both women stopped breathing.

Shelby stared at the mother, trying to find some clue in

her still face, but all she saw was discomfort. "I don't know," she said after thinking it over, because she didn't. She had heard talk at home of "white" and "colored" people, but no one had ever defined the terms for her.

The mother could take command now. The following question was easy. "Are you white?"

Shelby looked at her hand. It was dirty, but when it was clean, it was white. At any rate, the mother's encouraging tone seemed to want her to say so.

"Yes."

"Well," a redheaded woman with small eyes and sun-blasted skin said dryly, "white or not, she's lost, so you'd better get the telephone."

"I feel like a fool," the mother sighed, "telling them I have another lost child with the same name. But it's not the same child—it just doesn't make sense."

"Look," the sunburned woman snapped. "Watch," she said briskly to Shelby, "I'm not going to hurt you." She took a strand of Shelby's hair and rubbed it forcefully, then she lifted the strand and gave it a little tug. "You see, it's real gold, it didn't rub off. It's real hair—it stayed on her scalp. God may have given some coloreds light skin, but He never gave them blond hair. And those eyes! Does it make any sense now? That she couldn't be colored?" Shelby watched in awe as every jerk of the woman's arm tugged up her crisp navy-blue cotton shirt and revealed a sharp barrier of crimson between dry rust and creamy white.

"I suppose so," said the mother uncertainly. But she was still not completely convinced, perhaps because deep in her heart she knew that too many people had blended too many colors not to strike a combination that looked as real as the real thing.

The sunburned woman brushed her hands briskly. "That takes care of that. The other name probably wasn't Coles at all. Forget it and call the police. See you later—I've got things to do." She looked down at Shelby and clucked.

"Come on, dear," the mother said to Shelby. "We'll go to my house, and pretty soon someone will come to take you home."

"Will Mummy come?"

"No, a nice policeman will come and take you home to Mummy."

But Shelby knew the policeman would only get mad again because she and the puppy were still hanging around. And maybe he would ask her if she were colored and pull her hair harder and harder, pull it right out of her scalp, until she had no hair left at all. She began to cry bitterly at the thought.

The mother swept Shelby into her arms. The puppy clawed at the mother's skirt and whimpered, impatient to be carried too. And so they walked, and with the mother's scolding and the puppy's misbehaving and the mother's strong arms that felt like vises, Shelby was so frightened of what the mother might do to her and the puppy and what the policeman might do that she went limp and white, and mute.

She did not speak again for some time. A policeman came, not the one who was mad at her but a Santa Claus policeman—fat, ruddy, and kind-talking. He did not pull her hair or ask her if she was colored. But she would not talk to him or raise her eyes to him, not even when he petted the puppy and said that a dog was a fine friend who never let you get lost alone.

When they drove into the Oval, her name began to sing, soaring to a crescendo burst out of screen doors and running after the car on legs stout and thin, repeating itself over and over. There was no uncertainty. She had her identity back; she was Shelby, one and indivisible, a girl with real hair.

She sat up straight and looked out the car window, feeling her name caressing her face—"Shelby, Shelby, Shelby"—and seeing the waving hands like so many colored banners. For the first time in her short life she knew the joy of returning home after a journey among strangers.

The car stopped, and the police chief lifted Shelby out. The puppy prepared to follow, but Shelby gently pushed him back inside. She said softly, "This isn't really my doggie. He lost himself, and I found him. I think he's a white doggy, but I don't know. But please don't pull his tail to see."

The sayings of children were not easy to interpret, and he who took the time had time to waste. The police chief was too busy to ponder Shelby's words. "So this is the little fellow! Somebody called us about him this afternoon. I'll tell his folks you took good care of him. They'll be glad he had you for company. Now let's go show Momma you're safe." He took her hand and led her up the walk.

The small group of people on the lawn stared over her head at the chief, freezing their smiles, trying to chill him with cold silence. They let him pass without a handshake and then closed in behind him like sentinels on guard, as if to imply that they had to see the child safe inside before they would disperse. With Shelby safe, they could release the bitter gall they had swallowed for hours, not wanting to risk God's displeasure by mixing prayer with venom. Now that Shelby was whole and unharmed and God had presumably turned His ear to other emergencies they could unburden themselves of their grievances without fear of offending. It was rare in this bucolic summer resort off the coast of New England to feel a ripple of unease about the color of one's skin, and now it was as if a cold wet wind had blown through the community. On their way home to try to salvage what could be salvaged of the lost day, to try to unwind and restore summer's lost tranquillity, the Ovalites took turns at the dead horse.

"Show me one white man who can look at a colored man without saying to himself, I see a colored man."

"The only one I know of died on the cross, and the other one has not yet been born."

"I see white people all day long, from the time the milkman comes in the morning, and all I see is the man with the milk. After all, I don't want to marry him."

"Keeping us colored is one of their chief occupations. If they don't remember it every minute, they're afraid they'll forget we're not children of God."

"They must think they're God, that nobody can look like them but them."

"It's a wonder they ever found Shelby at all."

"They couldn't find a lost colored child, so they had to settle for any child that was lost. They had the whole town keeping an eye out—everybody put on dark glasses. Those of us with light-skinned children should put a tag on them, 'Please return to the colored race.' "

"They're the ones who make it so easy for us to pass. We jump their fences and they never find us, and all the time they're looking right at us."

By the time Corinne woke up from her sedation, Shelby had been long asleep. Corinne had lost a child for a day, and the strain of not knowing where Shelby was, or if she were even living or dead, had been more than her frail flesh could bear. The neighbors' account of Shelby's return gave her something to think about, as everyone knew who knew how she felt about color. If her feelings rubbed off on her children, they stood a good chance of catching white fear, and God help her if they decided to pass and were lost to her, not just for a day, but forever.

Shaking their heads and sighing, the Ovalites scattered to their cottages, returning to the slow domestic hum of daily routine refreshed by the break from the ordinary. They were secretly enjoying their ruminations now, anticipating the impact of their story on the beach the next day. Screen doors opened and were allowed to bang, and radios began to liven up the summer atmosphere. Makeshift suppers were made in kitchens, and little children began to be scolded as their mothers began to see them again as something less than angels on loan.

Inside the glassed-in porch, the chief of police presented Gram with her granddaughter, restraining his surprise that this old lady was as blue-eyed as the child who called her Gram. According to all his previous conceptions, her age consigned her to those generations that were sometimes less black but were never more white than they should be.

Gram rose up slowly from her chair. She read his thoughts, of course—so plainly were they stamped upon his face—and she dismissed his brand of thinking with a wave. She was immune to his lower-class mentality. Inherent in her was the Southern aristocrat's uncompromising contempt for poor whites, bred in the bone. She had never played with a poor white, supped with a poor white, or met a poor white on any level that was remotely social, the line of demarcation between their worlds sharper than the color line, which was openly crossed under cover of the night. Communication between white aristocrat and white trash was unknown, there being no magnet of color to attract one to the other.

"Well, here she is, safe and sound, and only a little the worse for wear," the chief said reassuringly.

Gram rose, holding herself as erect as an old gnarled stick that had rooted itself in time. In no one's memory had she ever not been old, not even in the memory of Corinne, who had been too young when Gram was not old to think of Gram as other than the rod and the staff that comforted her when Miss Josephine and Hannibal locked her out of their lives. Gram bent forward a little, not enough to upset her delicate balance, and stretched out her arms. Shelby's head burrowed into Gram's brittle old body, with its soothing smell of lavender. Gram spoke softly to the policeman, reserving her strength for getting Shelby to bed and calming her so that she could fall asleep. "Thank you for searching so long for my great-granddaughter. I thought this little town could be covered in an hour or so, except for the woods. But please convey the family's thanks to all you called in to help. The child's father, Dr. Coles, will send a check to whatever island charity you wish to name."

The Southern accent surprised him. Everyone else in the Oval spoke as well as he did. This old lady sounded like the colored maids who swarmed through town on their Thursdays off, looking for friendly colored faces and knowing better than to look for them in the Oval. This old lady did and yet somehow didn't talk with a tongue that was coated with grits and gravy. In fact, if she hadn't sounded so colored she would have sounded white, which was the nearest the chief could come to appraising the quality and inflection of a Southern gentlewoman's stubbornly unaltered pattern of speech. "Ma'am," he said, not sure that he meant to say "ma'am" with special deference, "we did our duty and were glad to. We don't want special thanks, but the doctor might be interested in helping our little hospital, which never has enough towels and washcloths. I'm sorry we didn't find your granddaughter sooner, but a little dog followed her all day, and nobody was looking for a little girl with a dog. I'm not making an excuse, ma'am, I'm just making an explanation." That was the way he meant to tell it to the reporter for the Vineyard newspaper when he came around to ask particulars. People believed what they read in that highly regarded weekly, which reached more homes than any Oval accusation, and would salve the town's conscience of any real or imagined guilt.

He began to walk backward toward the door, hearing the squeak, squeak of his policeman's shoes on the polished floor. He withdrew in this awkward manner not because it was his wont but because he found he could not tear his eyes from Gram's, gripped as he was by the implacable irony in them that seemed to strip him and pin him to the wall like a bug in a display case.

The other Ovalites would relent, would make a bitter joke, in time even forget in their unceasing effort not to be hypersensitive, a condition of mind which affected that very class of cooks with which they refused to acknowledge anything in common. But Gram, not having to ask herself if she were drawing a hasty conclusion because she was colored, could be unforgiving to the end, all of her blood rebelling against her private enemy, a white man whose actions in no way confirmed the superiority of race.

The door sighed after the chief. Gram took Shelby indoors, and Liz and the maids gave her bear hugs. The maids were smiling, but Liz was crying, though she didn't know why except that a younger sister was better to have around than not, no matter if she followed you around and got in your hair. The dog came on his belly to beg Shelby's pardon, and her endearments were the first kind words he had heard all day.

Then there was a hot bath. Shelby wanted Gram to bathe her; she usually demanded to be allowed to wash herself without assistance, but today she just didn't want to be alone. "Where's Mommy?" she asked, her little body covered in suds. When Gram told her that Mommy had felt so sad that the doctor had given her something to help her sleep, Shelby only said, "Oh, Gram, I'm so glad you made them let you stay awake."

After the bath there was a light supper in bed, which

Shelby was too tired to eat. Gram managed to feed her a few mouthfuls. Shelby didn't feel silly, she just felt glad to be Gram's baby. When the hot bath and the warm supper made it almost impossible for her to keep her eyes open any longer, she pushed sleep away until she could ask Gram the question that would not let go of her mind, no matter how hard she tried to shake it out of her head. Never before had she been forced to question who she was, who she really was, and the pain of not knowing threatened to tear her insides out by their roots. She was like an automaton, frozen in an eternal present of trembling palsy. Gram had grown aware of Shelby's tic and wondered what had happened that day to cause this little nervous reflex, but she refrained from making her little great-granddaughter aware of it.

Despite the warmth of being home, the clean, Ivory Soap smell of her body, the fresh feeling of hair brushed for the first time that day, the wonderful coziness of the bed, and Gram's face hovering close by, smiling down—despite all these solid assurances, she was still not sure of herself, as if some part of her were still lost, still trying to find its way back to before. She did not want to wake up in the morning to all the pleasure that Liz had promised her and have the day spoiled by a queer feeling of incompleteness.

"Gram," she said, staring hard, "am I colored?"

Gram's expression did not change. "Yes," she said, because there was no other answer, and to qualify it would not alter the fact but only confuse a child who preferred the simple truth.

Shelby's chest heaved with simple relief, not because she was black, but because she was something definite, and now she knew what it was. But a thought occurred to her, and she was anxious again. "Is Liz colored?"

"Yes."

"And Mommy?"

"Yes."

"And Daddy?"

"Yes."

"Are you colored too?"

"I'm your gram."

The answer satisfied Shelby. All the people she loved were like herself. "Oh, Gram, I'm so glad we're all colored. A lady told me I was white."

Shelby had been a child when she spoke those words, who spoke as a child and understood with a child's understanding. When she got lost, she was lost altogether, her identity deserting her, her name on doubting tongues, and her wholeness hanging by a tug of hair. There was no one to help her orient herself, and she could not communicate her need for help. In a world where everyone was adult and articulate, she was overwhelmed by the handicap of having to be a child. That she would ever coalesce into something concrete, with more sense than lack of it, seemed beyond the promise of prayer. She was still bits and pieces of other people: a frown she had no use for, a phrase stuck in a senseless sentence, a grunt like Gram's when the weather tied a knot in her back, walking like Gram when she had to place her hand on her hip to ease the pain of a rainy day, and echoing Liz's yeas and nays when half the time she felt just the opposite. Like most children, Shelby spent her days and hours trying on the most transparent parts of other personalities, gradually growing aware of their insufficiencies. Then slowly, at a snail's pace, and with a snail's patience, she would thread her frailties and fears, her courage and strength, her hopes and doubts, into the warp and woof that would cloak her naked innocence in a soul of her own.

Her walk through the woods had started out as a triumph of self, a beginner's step forward in independent action. But in her first adventure outside the concentric circles of her special world she had blended so completely with the passing crowds that she took on the color of their anonymity and could not find her way back to the road that separated the races. She walked in unreality, and no one gave her a clear, indisputable claim on herself until the Oval made her name a golden ball, tossing it from one mouth to another like seals having fun, with Gram letting it lie sweet on her tongue as if she could taste it. The joy of returning to kith and kin was greater than all her former joys. Love and likeness were equated in her mind. Never before in the Oval, which prided itself on its quiet ways, had Shelby seen such an outpouring of affection. She was everyone's heroine; not that she'd done anything—it was enough that she was Shelby, one of the children they cherished. It was enough that she was a precious little girl whom they did not want to lose to the woods, to the sea, to the other side of town, to some dark place where she would leave no trace behind, no solid object to bury in a vessel for their grief. She wanted to throw her arms around the Oval and all it contained—people, cottages, little parks, birds sunning themselves on the roof slopes in tidy little rows after their baths, and squirrels playing like perpendicular kittens up and down and through the trees.

For the first time in her life, Shelby saw this community as a whole. She did not want one face to change, one bird to fly away. She existed because they existed. Nothing was the same unless everything was the same; the interrupted heart never resumed its rhythm.

Shelby slowly became aware of Jezebel's excited barking. No, she was no longer six years old. She had been a child then, in the first embrace of belonging, equating love with order and homogeneity, identifying color as the core of character.

Now, through falling in love with Meade, she had been forced to admit that identity is not inherent. It is shaped by circumstance and sensitivity, and resistance to self-pity. The reality of the invisible spirit transcended the assumptions of the flesh, a great-grandfather she never knew might have said. Confrontation based on color had addled man since Moses married the Ethiopian woman and God made leprous the skin of the sneering man who challenged His right to move Moses to love.

Shelby loved Meade too much to listen to anybody who wished she loved him less. His parents, from all present signs, refused to acknowledge that they were gaining a daughter and not losing a son. Her own parents could not understand why only Meade could make her happy because, just as his parents had done with her, they had tagged him with a dictionary definition, looking him up under "Caucasian" and boxing him inside the words they found there, when there were a dozen other words that could also describe him. There *were* other men in the world, of course, but Meade was like no other. That was love's axiom and its paradox. Those who could not see what love saw must take it on faith that it was there. Meade had made Shelby the intimate of all his hopes and aspirations, pouring his mind into hers and encouraging her to shake off any thought of compromise. To ask for more from a man was to ask for too much. Wasn't it?

Shelby was well aware that her mother privately thought that she was throwing away her careful upbringing as a Coles, ignoring its obligations, dismissing its successes to live out a dream with a seed salesman's son. "How many people can play a piano?" her mother had openly asked her, answering herself immediately: "Practically anybody who has ever been a child. It is a standard parlor accomplishment. Most of the young men you grew up with could play a tune at a party from the time they were seven. But tell me how many of them were fool enough to give serious thought to expanding this frivolous skill into a full-time occupation that could support a daughter of the Clark Coleses in a manner approved by her parents?"

Shelby hadn't even bothered to answer her mother, for she knew she would never understand that she couldn't bear any of the men her parents saw as ideal suitors precisely because they paid more mind to who her parents were than to who *she* was. But Meade had never revered her as a sacred cow of the Coleses. She had been his girl, and her surname didn't matter because he planned to change it in due time. He wasn't marrying her parents. In fact she knew he saw them as the fat souls of a foolish generation, as dedicated to dead issues as were his own parents and their friends. With their meager ambition to succeed where success was assured, they crowded the un-creative highway to the good job, the good wife, the good life, the two point something children who had good col-lege prospects. They had no hunger, no goad of discon-tent. They had never gnawed in a wakeful night with a hunger to overreach the coming day's capacity.

He had held out his hand to Shelby and she had leaped the wide gap between all that she had been brought up to be and all that Meade was striving to be. She would have to learn to live with his brand of faith in a double union with man and musician, in a duality of discipline and desire.

Shelby sat up in her soft four-poster bed, stirred by her thoughts. She stroked the cotton sheets ruefully. Much as she loved her fiancé's idealism, his idea of a comfortable standard of living had little to do with her own, and would take some getting used to. She stretched her arms out to the open bay window. On such a balmy summer day, on this Elysian isle, anything seemed possible.

The sharp staccato rap of a knuckle at the door made Shelby wince. Once again Liz had beaten her out of bed. It was ever thus; even as little girls, Liz would scamper to the breakfast table and clamor for her morning meal, while Shelby could be made to budge only after the fiercest resis-tance. "You're awake?" her sister said, sweeping into the room with a sisterly lack of ceremony. "Did you hear Gram and me? We had quite a set-to. She wants to see you, but wait until you've had your coffee. I saw her on an empty stomach, and she made me feel queasy."

Shelby plumped the pillows behind her back and held out her arms for Laurie. "I could hear voices, but the Oval was already beginning to babble. What's wrong with Gram?" Liz handed Laurie over and curled up at the foot of the bed. The baby studied Shelby's face intently. She reached her little hand out for Shelby's bright hair, and her small round mouth shaped itself into a smile.

"Oh, she's perfect," Shelby sighed. "Did you ever see such glowing skin? I can never decide what color she is. Tan maybe, with pink showing through the surface. And the softest brown eyes in the world. I've always thought brown eyes were for tenderness. And I love her black hair; it's as black and shiny as a crow's wing in the sun. Oh, Liz, will all my children with Meade be fair? Can't one of them be Laurie's warm color?"

"I think it's going to be curly," Liz said contentedly. "Not plain old straight like mine, but a cross between Linc's and mine. She is a wonder child."

Shelby gently blew on Laurie's cheek. The baby's face puckered up and quivered. "Someday," Shelby whispered with mock solemnity, "some artist will capture this angel child on canvas and will win first prize at every exhibition."

Liz snorted. "Well, we'd win first prize for the fond and foolish, and Gram would be the first to say so."

Shelby remembered that Gram wanted to see her. "Do you know what's on her mind this morning?"

"I think she's *lost* her mind," Liz said flatly.

"Oh, Liz!" Shelby protested.

"Sorry. That was too harsh. But I do think Gram has suddenly gone senile, or is teetering on the brink. She had a dream or something about death, and now she thinks she's going to die. And she wants to go down South to do it, to the never-never land of magnolias, because long ago she lived in a house where nobody but slaves were my Laurie's color." Liz shrugged and half rose. "Oh well. I'd better go take my bath."

"Wait. You've a right to be impatient with Gram. She's been miserable about the baby. But I think that it's more that it's hard for her to accept her as a permanent member of the family without feeling replaced. All summer, everything's centered around the baby and the wedding. All of our talk has been about the future. It's made Gram retreat to the past. And the past may have confused her mind a little. She wants to go home because the old make their wishes dying wishes.

The young always think the old are wandering in their minds. They think that death is a word the old play with just to be cantankerous, as with a dangerous toy. Gram had stated the facts as she had studied them in her mind, and Liz and Shelby were turning them into fancies. Only Hannibal would have seen, he whose quiet joy had been to listen to Miss Caroline, who was always divided in his mind between the present and the epic past, he who had no blood bond of understanding but would have understood the homing heart's return to Xanadu, the separated flesh crying "take me" and both hands reaching out for help to return to the sweeter soil of memory. But Hannibal's black hand, his sympathetic hand, would have been of no use in her self-deception.

Liz snorted. "Gram will live to be a hundred. She's past the age for cancer or coronaries. And now she's getting too mean to die. She wants to pick up her marbles and go home. I guess it *is* easy enough for you to take Gram's side, now that you've become the apple of her eye, the hope for her future. I only hope your kids won't think they're better than Laurie because their father belongs to the chosen race."

Shelby blushed vividly at Liz's insinuation, and at her premature reference to parenthood. "Liz, I haven't any kids. At this moment, I haven't even got a husband. I didn't know you felt that way about Meade."

"What way? I didn't say how I felt. He's not for me, but I honestly think he is wonderful for you."

"Why isn't he wonderful for you?"

"Because I've got a man of my own."

"That's not what I mean, and you know it."

"Well then, to be crude about it, I just can't see a white man in bed. There's nothing about a white man that excites me. Maybe I put too much emphasis on sex, but that's what I think."

"Do you mean I don't put enough?" Shelby said sharply.

Liz groaned. "Here we go again. I was talking about me."

"Well, how do you feel about me?"

"I wouldn't have you any other way." Liz chuckled, a small smile flitting across her face.

"What does that mean?" Shelby demanded. "Tomorrow I'm going to be married, so please let's not be cryptic. Do you mean I'm cold?"

"Little virgin sister, don't *you* know?"

"How *could* I? . . . Oh!" gasped Shelby as she finally understood the meaning behind Liz's words. She blushed in surprise and embarrassment.

"You can ask the *obvious* question," Liz said kindly. Shelby took a deep breath. "Wouldn't you have married him even if you hadn't been sure?"

"Shelby, before I answer, will you remember something? You and I are two different people, neither of whom will always have the answer for the other. I'm your older sister, married, a mother, but still a long way from maturity. First off, I could never marry an artist. I wouldn't care *what* color he was. Popping out of bed because an idea popped into his head and leaving me high and very dry."

"But would that mean I was cold and didn't care? I thought it would mean I was understanding. Oh, Liz, now you've worried me."

"Don't be a ninny. Who says I know best? Who says I'm good for Linc? I don't seem to do very much of what he asks except go to bed with him, and after a while that may not be enough. I shouldn't have spent the summer here. I should have stayed in New York and cooked my husband's meals. I didn't come to this island for my baby's sake, I came because Mother has two maids. I was tired of being both of them at home."

"You're not lazy, Liz," Shelby said loyally.

"No, maybe not, but I'm not a real wife either. I'm still a lover girl, who thinks the rest of marriage is a drag. I'm as worried as you are for a very different reason."

"When Linc comes, won't he be here sometime today or

on the first boat tomorrow? Why not go back with him? The summer is almost over."

"Linc's not coming," Liz stated flatly, trying without success to hide her keen disappointment. "I called him last night to tell him about boat connections, but he wouldn't change his mind, as I'd hoped he would. So that, I regret to say, is that."

Shelby felt let down, but she said quickly, "Well, after all, Liz, my wedding's very important to me, but the clinic is very important to Linc. You two didn't have a fancy wedding, so I don't see why I should expect Linc to be excited about mine."

"No, maybe not, but he has exposed me to myself."

"Mother fits in there somewhere."

"He's not married to Mother. That's the whole point. I left home and Mother to marry him, and now I've come back."

"Does Linc expect you to give up your family?" Shelby asked in disbelief. "He's not that unfair."

"He thinks *I* am. I'm living in Mother's summer house, letting her support me."

"But Linc sent you money, for yourself and Laurie."

"Not enough to live in style in the very house Mother wouldn't let Linc be married in."

"Liz, don't exaggerate. Mother was planning your wedding up to the moment you eloped. She didn't expect you to substitute a stand-in."

"She expected Linc to substitute his friends who were doctors. She thought it was enough to have his mother coming from the stockroom at Macy's instead of a teacher's schoolroom. But she drew the line at his aunt and uncle. They are a cook and a butler. If their money was good enough to help him through med school, Linc thought they were good enough to see him get married. Since Mother didn't, I made Linc elope with me before he changed his mind about marrying into my stuck-up family. I'd had a hard enough time persuading him to propose to a Coles. If you'll forgive me for gloating, I think it serves Mother right that Meade's family has thumbed their noses at her. In fact, I think it's perfectly lovely."

The day Liz had proposed to Linc and was accepted, she was skeptical about waiting until summer to marry him in the Oval, even though in her teenage years she had romanticized about such a day and constantly demanded that her mother cross her heart in consent. In the months between proposal and performance, her mother found a thousand ways, little and big, subtle and blunt, to pressure her into considering the consequences of marrying somebody nobody knew, that is to say, nobody anybody knew. Her mother blew the trumpet of praise for marriage to her own kind, if not color, the right color being preferable but not as mandatory as the right class. That class and the posture it demanded had given her the self-assurance to feel that no barrier was insurmountable, and to say with ease that she looked white but wasn't.

Liz recalled that during their courtship Corinne had delicately suggested that she was seeing too much of Linc to the exclusion of more social young men. It wasn't fair to let him think that she was serious when, of course, such a serious young man might keep her from having the fun her youth entitled her to have. Linc had known very well that he and Liz might never have met, or at least might never have progressed beyond introduction had they met at some charity affair that one of his more socially ambitious doctor friends had bludgeoned him into attending. That their meeting was professional got him started on a footing that did not scare him off. They met in an operating theater and fell into casual conversation. Linc introduced himself, and Liz's name, when she said it, made him instantly aware that she was one of the Coleses for whom he had a great deal of professional admiration. He knew that all Coleses and their sons were doctors, and now apparently their daughters were too.

Liz was just beginning her internship at the hospital where Linc was in heart research. That Liz had entered medicine was indeed in keeping with the Coles tradition. Since Clark and Corinne had no son to propagate the faith, Liz had always known that she, the elder daughter, could follow no other course. After her marriage to Linc, however, Liz had given up medicine, choosing the more traditional roles of wife and mother instead.

The baby had fallen asleep in Shelby's arms, lulled by the rise and fall of her breast. One hand had curled around Shelby's finger, and Shelby's eyes grew tender with compassion at the sight. After four months of life on earth, the long span of years to come still had cast no shadow. Shelby looked up at Liz. She knew she should somehow defend Meade's parents, even if she felt a funny twinge in her side at the thought. "Liz, do you have to be so honest? Meade's parents weren't crude about it. They begged to be excused with polite regrets and a present. If their explanation was an out, at least it wasn't outright rude. Meade says his father does have high blood pressure, and the long trip here at this time of the year wouldn't help it any. Meade made the joke, a bitter joke, that our wedding plans had probably put him in bed for a week. And of course it wasn't really a joke. In his wildest nightmare I'm sure the poor man never had a dream about Meade getting married to a colored girl. If he had to sit through the real thing it might be more than that blood pressure could bear. He'd likely go into shock."

"Well, I think it's just a beautiful thing that you can be so understanding," Liz said wryly. "When I pinch myself, I don't feel colored. I just feel the hurt of it—maybe that's what being colored means for most of us. You feel the hurt of it."

Liz got up from the foot of the bed and went to the window. She stared out at the Oval. She had loved it so in her childhood, this safe, contained world where she had come every summer except for the summer past when her marriage and two-week honeymoon and getting settled into her small flat gave her no time to wish she were here. But when Laurie was born in April, and the flat seemed smaller and the Harlem streets noisier, then the sentiment grew in Liz that Laurie should spend her first summer on earth in the quiet Oval, in a large convenient house where gracious living was taken for granted.

She had asked Linc to join her for two weeks in August to share the week's gaiety preceding the wedding and the restful week following it, when her mother would take charge of the baby and free her and Linc to do what they pleased, when they pleased. But Linc said without apparent regret that he couldn't afford a vacation. The first year of their marriage, after the expense of furnishing a flat and adding a member to their family, had put a considerable strain on their by no means endless supply of money. When Liz had countered that his vacation would cost him nothing but his fare, he reacted as if she had insulted him by offering him her family's hospitality, refusing to see it as the gesture of reconciliation that he was in no way ready to accept. And now he was not even coming for the day of the wedding, despite the pleas in her letters and phone calls, even if it meant embarrassing her before her Ovalite friends. They thought they could easily guess why he had no wish to insert his dark face into the family picture.

With her back still turned to Shelby, Liz said quietly, "When I knew I was going to have a child, I wasn't happy about it. I wasn't ready to be a mother. I wanted more time to be a bride. Then Laurie was born, and I was ready to resent her. They brought her to me and put her in my arms, and I saw that she was brown. She was a completely colored child, without the protective coloring of the Coleses. I can't tell you how much I loved her at that moment. I wanted to fight the whole white race for her. She looked too small and helpless to fight it alone." She let out a deep breath. "But in the nature of things she must. It's a private and internal struggle. And to win she will have to fight back without bitterness, not replacing her hurt with hate but letting that hurt enrich her experience."

She faced around to Shelby. "There's a bitterness in Linc against whites, against near whites, as he thinks of our kind, against anyone with whom he's never related socially. But I sometimes wonder if Linc isn't confusing class with color, or using old yardsticks to make his judgment. He can't accept unless he sees, and race relations and class distinctions and color differences are too subtle for any dim view of them."

Laurie stirred and kicked in her sleep. "He didn't take a dim view of you," Shelby said with a smile.

"That's because he insists I'm exceptional. He isn't ready to admit I'm standard Oval product, no better, no worse than the friends I grew up with. He can't divorce me from my family. I'm everything that's gone into making me, and that includes Mother, who might even have beat me to bed with Linc if she had met him first."

Shelby rolled her eyes resignedly. "Liz, I wish you wouldn't, but you always will. You're only guessing about Mother. There's nothing you really know."

"I had bigger ears than you when we were kids, and more interest in the sex life of my elders. I'm pretty sure I know about Mother. And I know I know about Dad, time and place."

For a moment there was silence in the room, except for the sounds of the Oval rising in fuller volume outside the window, responding to the perfect day. Shelby stared at Liz just as she used to when they were children and Liz had a secret to tell about the mysterious ways of adults. Somehow Liz's secrets seemed to sap some of the joy from growing up, driving her to her family of dolls as the only sphere of order and understanding she knew.

Liz grimaced with an attempt at insouciance that neither believed. "When Linc and I were on our honeymoon cruise, we saw Dad and Rachel on one of our stopovers. They were across the room in a restaurant, looking like lovers in spite of Dad's fifty and Rachel's surely forty years. I thought their affair had dwindled away to nothing, that they were a couple of old shoes, with no romantic nonsense between them, but there they were. Anyway, they didn't see us. And I got away fast before Linc could see them. Told him I'd had too much sun and felt sick to my stomach. When you see your own father with the other woman it has that effect."

But Shelby hadn't had the jolt of seeing her father at fifty in youth's arena. She didn't believe that reflective middle age would allow itself to flirt with irrevocable folly. At most, she thought her father was guilty of a brief excursion in self-deception. "All you really saw, Liz, was Dad in a moment of nostalgia before you and Linc could make him a grandfather. He didn't do anything fatal to Mother, like falling in love with somebody much younger. He had a holiday with Rachel, who's never been a threat to Mother's marriage. They were probably more wistful about the past than expectant about the future. Nobody's been hurt. Mother doesn't know, and Dad's settled down to being a grandfather."

Shelby suddenly remembered a dance she had been to back home in New York. Her escort for the evening was a young intern whom her father knew well. The dance was a fashionable charity affair in a fashionable hotel downtown that had found, after years of viewing them with alarm, that colored people with money spent more of their money than whites with more money to spend.

To Shelby and her escort there had been too many of the middle-aged on the dance floor trying to make up for the years when they could not afford to dress up in diamonds and go to expensive places. Their faces fell apart before the evening was half over, and everything rebelled, their feet, their heads, their backs, even their smiles that had to work harder and harder to amount to anything.

Corinne had been there, as she usually was, though Clark always seemed to take these occasions to have a last-minute emergency call. He and Rachel would drive somewhere distant and dine and dance in some little roadhouse where the management would make the prudent decision that it was better to serve a mixed couple, as the two appeared to be, than face a lawsuit the defendant would probably lose. The other diners invariably found more of interest in Clark and Rachel than in the dinners they were letting dry up on their plates. They were pretty sure what the score was with these two. They knew where they would go when they left, and what they would do when they got there. It was written on their faces.

It was true that something was written on their faces, but it was not the obscene leer of desire but a deep relishing of the intimacy of dinner for two in a place where no one knew them and no one would run and tell. They were grateful for whatever their love was allowed. It had not been allowed a beginning before that uncertain hour on a day without a date in a year they could never agree on when Rachel's doorbell rang and there was Clark, a drink or two inside him but not drunk.

He had come inside her door and stood there staring,

taking in the beauty of her brownness, which was like no other. A paler woman pales by comparison. Not everyone can see it, but those who can know there is no beauty like that of a brown-skinned woman when she is beautiful: the velvet skin, the dark hair like a cloud, the dark eyes like deep wells to drown in. He said her name softly, caressing her with it, and she was helpless. She began to tremble, and she could not hide it. It was like nakedness. He saw it, and he took her in his arms, and all the yielding that Corinne had denied him was in her incredible softness as if her body had melted into his. So it began, without a beginning, even if afterward they told each other that there had been a period of courtship, each wanting so much to believe that there was more to it than an hour of undammed physical lust. Not flags waving, perhaps, but perhaps other signs, secret yet unmistakable, and building up like an orchestra tuning up, each instrument unrelated until the fusion of triumphant sound established an eternal empathy, reechoing through time.

Meanwhile, at the charity dance Corinne had given most of her dances to dark men. She liked it best when the lights were dim and the tempo slow, and the dark hand on her back pressed into her bare flesh, drawing her closer, audaciously closer, to the point of contact. And the ball of fire would burn between them until the music stopped, the lights came up, and Corinne walked decorously back to her box, her escort's hand lightly touching her elbow. Many eyes would follow her because she was one of the Coles wives, and thus in this small circle truly above reproach.

Clark would soon come to fetch her, and he and Corinne

would ride home with their minds miles away. Both of them would hear other voices, and neither of them could reach out to the other for any understanding of their common compulsion.

Liz was a realist and could therefore accept the truth of her parents' infidelities, but Shelby could not. "What makes you think Mother doesn't know?" she scoffed. "Wives know what their husbands are made of better than trusting daughters. Until last summer I never suspected that Dad's been dividing his vacation between Mother and Rachel ever since we discovered that boys were more fun than fathers and didn't need a month of Dad to have a happy summer. But I never did believe that he went off on a two-week fishing trip with some white sawbones each year just because he liked to go fishing; I just thought he was getting his kicks going places with white guys that he couldn't go with colored. And all the time Dad was somewhere with Rachel, which makes a world more sense to me. As for Laurie aging his libido, I bet he's champing for Mother to get this wedding over with so he can pop off someplace with Rachel for the last few days of his vacation."

Shelby sat up in bed with a grimace. "Listen, Liz, maybe I am a big fool. Maybe I'm just a dumb blind baby. But you know what?" Her eyes narrowed, and she jabbed her index finger at Liz like a knife. "I think only seeing the bad, only poking fun, only trying to lift up the rug and look for bugs underneath is its own kind of blindness. You hear me? You ever look around Strivers' Row growing up, or the Oval?" She swept her arm in front of her in an arc. "I didn't see a lot of kids we knew whose parents looked after them any better than ours. I look at Mother and Father and I see two people who've been good and kind and loving to us from the day we were born. We ever gone hungry? We ever needed for anything? Mother and Father may well have looked elsewhere for some things they couldn't give each other, but I'd like you to tell me what that means to us, next to everything else." Shelby's pale eyes flashed wildly, and her uncombed blond hair—the hair whose color had caused her so much grief as a child—coiled itself around her head like a clutch of snakes.

Liz chuckled dryly and took a step backward. "Easy, little sister." She drew the words out slowly. "Easy. You're wrong if you think I'm not grateful for everything we've been given. Lord knows, it's more than most, and it didn't come by luck. Just because it's 1953, not 1853, doesn't mean it's that much less dangerous to be colored, and when we take the new car out I get more looks from our own kind than from whites. It's easier to hate your own kind for what they have than to hate somebody far away for what you don't. But, as glad as I am that we always had nice things as children, I'll be damned if I'm going to eat that dish of humble-pie gratitude every day of my life, and let it blind me to things that aren't right. When something's wrong it's wrong, and all the maid-cooked dinners in the Oval won't change that fact."

Shelby slapped her hands down on the bed. "No, Liz, that's not my point. You don't see—"

"No!" Liz cut Shelby off with a wave of her hand. "If I

have to listen to you tell me how ungrateful I am, you *will* hear *me* out too. Tell me that all those years you looked without seeing, listened without hearing. You're quick to hit me with all the good lessons we learned from our parents, and God knows we did—hard work, pride, and manners, manners for every step we took in a day—but now I guess it would be beyond belief for you to think you might have learned some bad ones too? Did it ever occur to you that there may be more of a tie between what you saw from Dad and what you see in Meade than you'd like to admit? I know myself I wonder at times how I can even bring myself to trust a black man, but I'll tell you, it feels like the sex and the doubt get all tied up with each other in my chest, and I can't tell one from the other."

Shelby threw the sheets off her legs and swung herself onto the floor. She paused as if to speak, her face twitching with emotion, but then she thought better of it. She shouldered her way past Liz to the door.

"Shelby, wait. I'm sorry."

Shelby clutched tightly at the doorknob, the veins popping in her forearms. She paused for a heartbeat and then swung the door open. Stale air rushed in from the hot, unventilated hallway. She twisted her neck to regard her sister. "You're so proud of how much you think you know, Liz. Well, you don't know everything, and you don't know anything about my love for Meade. *You* might not trust black men; that's *your* problem."

Liz turned her palms out in supplication. "Shelby, that's not what I meant."

"Oh, yes, it is!" Shelby hissed, her words slicing the air like a razor. "How dare you, on the eve of my wedding, imply that I'm turning my back on my race?" Her voice caught and she ran into the hall, a flick of her wrist slamming the door tightly shut behind her.

CHAPTER EIGHT

*A*t the moment Shelby's door closed, Clark Coles placed his bare foot on the Oak Bluffs beach to begin his morning walk into town. The ferry landing was behind him, and he could just make out a boat in the distance, coming with a fresh brace of day trippers from Cape Cod. Clark hunched his shoulders against a chill wind blowing in off the water and stooped to roll his left pants leg up a little farther. He cherished these walks; lately they seemed to be his only chance to get away from the hubbub of the wedding. He stopped at a thin white pole that was listing to one side. Pushing it upright with two hands, he swept his foot through the sand to fill in the hole he had created so the pole would stay upright. It was a funny thing, these poles, the way they divided the beach. Corinne would always meet her friends at the twelfth pole, but Shelby and her young group always congregated around the nineteenth, and the young married couples put down their blankets even farther up. Clark guessed that Shelby and Meade would move up themselves next summer—that is, if they came to the island at all.

Clark shook his head. He would never have chosen Meade as a likely mate for his daughter, but it hadn't seemed of late that he'd done a particularly good job choosing a bride himself, so he guessed he couldn't speak as an authority. He glanced at a gnarled piece of driftwood and stepped around it. At least she seemed happy. Was Clark that happy the day before he married Corinne? He honestly couldn't remember. He put his hands in his pockets and rubbed his fingers together. That really wasn't a fair question, he thought, since people today seemed to marry based on a whim, based on some here-today-gone-tomorrow flight of fancy, without a glance at the more practical considerations that seemed to mean everything in Clark's day. The reasons his daughter had for choosing Meade were so different from his and Corinne's that the single word "marriage" seemed insufficient to describe both events, lacking the flexibility to stretch to both poles.

Clark shook his head again. It had all happened so fast. He and several other Northern-educated doctors young enough to be altruistic had accepted an invitation to attend a month-long series of panels on modern techniques in medicine at the college where Corinne's father Hannibal was president and Corinne reigned as campus queen.

Clark had been automatically given access to the highest circles of the society in which he found himself. He had all the proper credentials, coming as he did from a family of physicians, all of whom, including his father, were sons of fair Harvard. As the youngest of three brothers, all successful general practitioners who lived prosperously on Strivers' Row in Harlem (a street so called because of the prominence and pretensions of this envied and imitated group of professional men and their pretty wives), he was determined to excel in any area that offered a challenge. He was the first of his family to get an office in a white doctors' building downtown, obtained through strings pulled by a fellow grad of Harvard Medical School, and he was on his way to becoming a brilliant diagnostician. He was beginning to gain recognition from some of the top men in his field, and he had a growing pool of patients who were willing to ignore his race to avail themselves of his talents. Those of his white patients who did not know that he was colored were not too dismayed when they learned it; they decided, as whites generally did, that he was an exception to the general run of his race, a freak, a flash of lightning that would probably not strike his generation again, their knowledge of the colored man and his genes being limited to the creations of their cooks.

Clark's brothers had married attractive, educated women who had given them sons clearly destined for Harvard as well, as evinced by the little crimson emblems sewed on their tiny sweaters. Clark meant to marry better and have at least one more Harvard-bound son than his brothers. His brothers had all chosen Northern brides, but Clark had a theory, by no means original, that the South produced the colored woman nonpareil. Washington was generally accepted as the place to start the search, the charm and beauty of its women attributed to generous infusions of the blood of senators, men who, though rarely beautiful or charming themselves, managed with the help of their colored mistresses to produce exceptional qualities in their children and their children's children. Yes, the rarefied nature of Washington women was a legend in sophisticated colored circles.

When Clark met Corinne, then, it was a meeting of two perfect people. She was the daughter of a college president, and he could never hope to marry better than that. But neither of them was interested. In Sabina, Corinne's brown classmate, Clark had found the perfect girl-woman, and he wanted to marry her. He had not had time for love before, and until he met Sabina he had never experienced the emotion that is blind to color lines and racial bars and class divisions and religious prejudices and all the other imposed criteria that have nothing to do with love but have so much to do with marriage.

For ten blissful days he saw Sabina whenever their time coincided, and each meeting was a fresh discovery of her sweetness. Her color never crossed his mind except in admiration, and her scholarship status, and the simple background that it implied, made him want to give her more than she had ever had. He knew that he had found his girl, and he was almost as sure that he had found his wife. At the unforeseen perfect moment before he returned to New York he intended to propose. He would need all the time he could get in between to pray that she would not refuse.

He could not know that a campaign was planned behind his back to wean this very eligible visitor away from a lowly scholarship student and match him with someone better. And of course there was no one better than Corinne, who was his peer in all the important details, those ironclad facts of background that made the fundamentals of love seem secondary. Every blue-veined hostess was pressed into giving a party for the visiting doctors. In the roundabout parlance of politeness, Sabina was not expected at any party. She would not cry foul and claim that she had been deliberately ignored, nor in all fairness could she. She was just one of the many students who did not even know the people who were having the affairs. There wasn't any issue, and to create one would have been unthinkable.

As a visitor from the North, with an imposed obligation to represent the section, the class, the culture from whence he had come, Clark had no gracious way of rejecting the seemingly good intentions of his hosts to display their fabled hospitality. In keeping with the spirit of giving, an animated bouquet of the year's most popular debs was presented to the visiting doctors as dates for the duration. It was inevitable, it was arranged, that Clark would draw Corinne out of the nonexistent hat, for to everyone except themselves their coming together had the full consent of heaven.

Though no one agreed more than Gram, she thought it the better part of wisdom to give heaven human assistance. In June, Corinne would graduate, and whatever restraints within which Gram held her because of school and study would be in effect no longer. Corinne would come into the ripeness of her twenty-first birthday amid the full-blown summer of the South, which boiled the blood more than the meager summer of the North. Gram was already past seventy, and weary of the night watch. She was quietly resolved to see Corinne married to this mannerly, fair-colored doctor before she had time to make a misstep in the dark of some deep wood with some dark man who would not even try to break her fall. In the long, bedeviling summer of the South, a yielding woman without benefit of miracles could bear the child of many fathers. Gram wanted to see her settled up North, where the ruling passion was ambition and men sought the smile of success more than the favors of love, finding this gilded goddess more fruitful with her golden children than the most abundant woman.

Gram cut her plan of action to the order of Corinne's vanity. She never dwelled on the merits of marriage. Indeed, she had never seen in her own limited relations with Augustus or Josephine's dismal journey into Nirvana anything to recommend marriage as a union of loving hearts in which much was given and much was received. In Corinne's childhood years, the years of dolls and simple pleasures, Gram had never let herself look ahead to the time when Corinne would come into consciousness of herself as a woman, whose logical counterpart was man. Gram had lived without a man in bed beside her, and so had Josephine. Hannibal had always been too buried in someone else's history to care about his own family's future, but Gram cared, and while she knew that Corinne could never marry white, she allowed herself to hope against hope that she'd never marry colored either. But when Corinne reached her riper teens, and boys and clothes and the blossoming of her own beauty became her feverish concern, Gram saw what Hannibal was too preoccupied to see, seeing only Miss Caroline in the aging, worn image of Gram whenever he took the time to look over his glasses. Gram saw that all the dried-out, arrested passion in Hannibal, and in Josephine, and in herself whose life in love had been brief and unrewarding—spent as it was with a man too sorry for himself to give joy to a woman—all that unspent passion had somehow seeped into the blood of this young woman and was now biding its time until it exploded.

Even in Corinne's early teens, when a child, though a child, can still bear a child, Gram had been forced to play the role of watchdog duenna, reluctantly reigning dowager in the circle of mothers at parties. She never trusted Corinne to go home with a servant, who could be bribed or cajoled into letting her slip through her fingers. As the better part of wisdom, Gram was forced to encourage Corinne to entertain at home, where she could keep watch in a nearby room, shooing her granddaughter back into a lighted parlor whenever she wandered toward the dark outdoors with a brown boy at the ready (though far from ready for responsibility) breathing hard behind her. That Corinne remained above reproach until the day she married Clark was due in no small part to Gram's unremitting vigilance, and to the obsessive fear it bred of getting caught with a dark boy's baby.

Corinne walked in virtue, but everything in her walk, and in her voice, and in her eyes was a promise of pleasure to come. She seemed the cream of women, a woman who had much to give but who would not squander it, bred from birth to keep it intact for the man she would marry. She would grace his home with her charm and beauty and she would make his bed joyous, all without ever having to shame his hearth with another man's memory of her shamelessness.

And so she bided her time, waiting for marriage to release her from the cage of her ignorance, to give her the right to make bold inquiry. Then she could free that second self, the dark devourer, the primitive behind the pale skin.

Gram did not know and could not have imagined the size of the monster that stalked Corinne, or the multifold shapes it would assume. All that Gram knew about girls who couldn't wait was what she had seen when a weeping coed was whisked off campus before her rounding belly brought open disgrace to the school. To Gram, the lesson to be learned was that some girls should marry young or come to grief as unwed mothers. Where the embarrassing problem of sex reared its head, the only place to solve it was the marriage bed. Gram's iron will ensured Corinne's restraint, and it also ensured that Clark would not escape from her orbit. Another colored generation would claim a share of Gram's blood, but with her willing it; better to see that blood in the fair-tinted face of a child born with God's blessing than turn to ink in a child turned black as the devil whose thrust had spawned it.

The final end-of-the-season party of the frenetic social whirl that had embraced Clark might have been designed for Gram's purpose. The slightly hyperthyroid hostess put all her captive guests through all the ingenious tortures that an all-night party can inflict, winding up the program with scrambled eggs at seven. When Clark brought Corinne home, obviously tired and clearly showing that she was also tired of Clark, Gram surmised at once that nothing had happened, nothing bad of course, but nothing good either. They had a lackluster look to them, nothing like the aura of two people in love. Their feet were too tired from dancing to walk on air, and their heads were too heavy with sleep to care about clouds.

Gram got rid of Corinne by packing her off to Hannibal's study to let him see that his only child had returned to the fold neither maimed nor molested. These extremes had not even occurred to Hannibal, who had slept untroubled throughout the night, unaware that his daughter's virgin bed was empty of its occupant. When she entered his private world he was having breakfast from a tray, a history book propped in front of him. Politely and absently he listened to Corinne, praising her pretty dress; he drew no significance from the hour of its attire. Corinne's voice fell on his ears like the sound of a distant skirmish to a restless sentry, and her image was blurred by the sight of the printed page in front of him.

Alone with Clark, Gram inclined her head toward a chair, and she and Clark sat together in the formal hallway. They both kept their backs ramrod straight, Gram to hold her tired old body together, Clark to keep from falling asleep in the quiet after the long night's clamor. They faced each other across their worlds, the bridge between them lowered for the crossing when Gram permitted Clark to sit in her presence. The significance of her dispensation escaped him, though his easy compliance did not escape her. Spearing Clark's eyes with her own, Gram refused to let her mind succumb to weariness until Corinne's future was settled.

Clark braced himself for a dressing down; no doubt this grandam had put two and two together and made the usual error in that kind of nasty, half-cocked addition. It was true enough that some busybodies were trying to make a romance out of his dates with Corinne, forgetting or ignoring the fact that they had been no more to each other than names in a hat. This old lady had probably heard the gossip, which was always two-headed when heard third or fourth hand. And since he had shown no evidence of honorable intentions, made no call on Corinne's father, made no mention of Corinne's meeting his family, he could understand that an anxious grandmother, looking at him in evening clothes in the morning hours, might suspect a wolf underneath the fancy trappings.

She didn't know her granddaughter, he thought to himself. She could handle herself. He hadn't got to first base with her. He hadn't really worked on it, but they were both young and the moon was bright and her lips had barely responded to the kiss he supposed she was expecting when he brought her home from a party. In fact, she seemed to have a thing for dark men. At least she gave them most of her dances. He was lucky if he got her first dance and her last. He didn't mind admitting that he wasn't good at shaking a leg; it made him feel self-conscious, like making love in public. But surely Corinne didn't expect to dance her way through life. Didn't she know that a doctor's hand held as much skill as a dancer's feet? Not that he wanted her to admire him. Not that he wanted her to get serious about him. But he couldn't help but feel piqued that he had made so little impression on her. She was pretty enough to be a challenge to any man, and he was male enough to wish he could boast to his friends that he could have had a college president's daughter for the snapping of his fingers, except that she was second string to a girl named Sabina.

Sabina . . . He had demanded more than was fair of her understanding. But he had fallen in love with her because there was empathy between them, this communication that silence and separation couldn't alter. She would forgive him this innocent defection. He, who had squandered so much of her patience, was impatient to hear her say that he had not. But for Sabina's sake he could not leave until this old woman's unconvinced eyes believed the simple truth that nothing had been created between himself and her granddaughter that could not be ended now and forever. He searched his mind for words that would make clear this total absence of design without being inelegant or ungallant. When they were said and accepted, he would leave their lives with the assumption that he would be forgotten before the falling of the leaves.

"Young man," Gram said, "are you in love with my daughter?"

Every thought that Clark had collected flew out of his mind. He felt his face redden like a schoolboy's. "Whatever my feelings," he said wildly, "I'm sure your granddaughter is not in love with me."

"How do you know, young man? Have you asked her?"

"Of course not, ma'am, I wouldn't ask such a conceited question."

"Nonsense! The world wouldn't last very long if everyone were as bashful as you."

That stung him. "I'm not a boy, I'm twenty-eight,

ma'am. I'm also a doctor. I could hardly claim to be bashful before women. But I'm also a gentleman. I respect your granddaughter's right to choose for herself without persuasion."

"And if she chose you?"

He could think of nothing else to say, so he muttered miserably, "I would be honored."

Gram rose. "I'm very tired, young man. I hope you'll excuse me. I'm old, past seventy. I don't expect to live forever. I want to see my motherless granddaughter settled before I die." She tried to think of his first name: "Carl" or "Clark" or something beginning with C. But it didn't matter, thank God; he too could be called Doctor.

Clark proposed to Corinne after two weeks of escorting her places. In the fourth week a date was set, invitations were sent out, a wedding dress selected, and all the other arrangements of a spectacular happening put in place. The wedding was accomplished without a hitch.

Clark shook himself from his reverie and looked at his watch. He was running late; he had errands to run for Corinne. What was done was done. He was fifty-two. Twenty-four years was long enough for any man to have to live with a mistake. He turned and headed for home, soothed by the thought that if all went as planned his time of penance was almost at an end.

CHAPTER NINE

*I*f in Gram's distorted eye Liz's baby Laurie was a carbon copy of Hannibal, if in Liz's biased eye Laurie was the wonder child of the world, an impartial eye presented with an album of Laurie's ancestors might have lingered longest on a tintype of a preacher, Preacher Coles, born a slave around the time that Gram was born the daughter of blue-blooded slave owners, living and dying without ever knowing that Gram existed, but cofounder of the same family nonetheless.

Preacher was the first of the Coleses who was called to heal, carrying his gift across seven counties, seeking the one in which he would settle. All he possessed was the shirt on his back and the Bible in his hand that he couldn't read, though he turned the pages and made as if he could, and preached a mighty word.

He had a voice that was like no other, a cello, a flute, a clap of thunder. A copper-colored man with wild auburn curls shot through with red strands, he looked the way he talked, like an angel of the lord, like a flaming sword. He could take words and turn them into pictures that brought the whole of heaven within soul's reach. There wasn't a sinner he couldn't save. There wasn't a cabin that didn't welcome him, or a chicken's neck that wasn't wrung for him, or a daughter who wasn't paraded before him.

He was twenty when he got the call. He was working in the fields, and he put down his hoe, took his Bible in his hand, and began to walk with God. All the time he walked he was looking for a land of plenty, and a strong-built woman who could bring a child to birth without dying in labor and leaving it motherless. He had seen so much dying. He had stood beside his stricken parents, powerless, watching as they were struck down, the fever burning them to the bone. The herbs hadn't helped, nothing helped. He lived, but his younger sisters and brothers, four of them, four rickety stair steps, had been born to die, some before walking or talking, or even really knowing they were alive. Preacher himself had been spared, in part because half of his blood was the blood of his mother's master, a hard-drinking Irishman who had broken his mother's hymen by divine right upon purchasing her, before mating her with one of his bucks to increase his herd of livestock, which recurring plagues were depleting. Preacher received his inheritance in his begetting: enough white blood to immunize his colored blood against the white man's pestilences that killed off his ma and then his pretend pa, and then his brothers and sisters, one after one, until there were none.

He had walked away from the plantation after the death of his family, and no one tried to stop him. The South was at war, and hunger was dogging the army's heels. A runaway slave was one less mouth to feed. Preacher lived each day as it came, sleeping where nightfall found him, running errands for the promise of a penny, buying penny buns if the promise was kept and begging at back doors for bacon rind when the need for meat became a craving. With a stick and stealth and stolen matches, he learned to catch wild creatures. He grew older and began to work for a dime a day chopping wood, or picking cotton, or plowing. With his stick handy for rabbit stew, and plenty of old sheds scattered about in which to make a bed, it was enough.

He survived. He did not succumb to pellagra, or coughing sickness, or any of the other crippling afflictions that spread through the region as food got harder and harder to come by. When he ailed, he holed up like a hurt dog, sometimes going two or three days without food, without water, lashed by diarrhea and nausea, sometimes wandering in his head. There was no hand anywhere to help him, but somehow he always came back to his senses, finding a stream to wash away his stink. He would cup the healing water in his cleansed hands, drinking it slowly like wine. The wine gave him strength to seek bread, and the bread and the wine restored his wholeness. He had the will to stay alive. He knew he got the will from God; all the singing and praying he had ever listened to gave God the power of life over death in him.

One place Preacher worked was a small, shabby parsonage, whose parson had the look of a man to whom every penny counted. Preacher asked for his pay in a Bible book. The parson wasn't much for giving niggers books, but it suited his pocketbook better than wages. There were three or four old Bibles in the attic, worn, torn, and past pulpit use. He would fetch the one with pictures, for it would teach this ex-slave better than words could that God and everybody else with a soul were white.

When he was twenty or thereabout, Preacher found his promised land and a strong-built woman who owned a piece of it. She made her living by taking in washing, but her land had been pastureland, rich with sheep droppings. It could permit a man with a mind and a back to work it. The woman owned it legally, a legacy from her mother, who had received it from Old Sir when emancipation freed him to prove his spoken word by written deed.

The woman was Old Sir's daughter, born in his later life, when the children of his marriage were grown, their mother gone, and his grieving over. Though his big house was empty without a second wife, no willing woman of his own kind persuaded his eye like the slave girl he bought in a bundle of field blacks, testing her arm for its soundness and being himself enslaved by its softness.

There was no hiding his infatuation. He gave her no work but to wait for his coming, and she kept to her cabin in the quarters. The bucks knew better than to go near her, and the women slaves shunned her because her seduction did not shame her, nor did the bright-skinned baby at her breast. At war's end, freedom enabled Old Sir to openly keep his concubine in a style beyond anything she had been accustomed to. Even though his own life was in shambles, and his fortune in shreds, he had a house built for her before he even counted the cost of putting his own house together again for the son who was heir to it.

The woman, the ebony woman, was as pleased as if she had moved into the house of her dreams, for she had never dreamed of dwelling in marble halls. The house had three rooms, one for sleeping, with a closet, bless God, and a chest of drawers; another room for cooking, with a stove and a sink and a pump in the sink that could fill a bucket as many times as one was set under it. Hanging from a nail on the outside kitchen wall was a big round tub that could with some contortion hold a body for an all-over wash. The third room was a parlor just for sitting, with easy chairs to do the sitting in and a fireplace to make the winter bearable. The outhouse was built from new, sweet-smelling wood, and a bag of lime with a scoop beside it was there to keep it that way.

No carriage wheels raised the dust outside this idyllic void that Old Sir had created. This quiet ebony woman, her features as chiseled as a queen's face on a coin, holding their butternut child who would contentedly suck the candy sticks he brought her, was every man's dream of a woman. Without books to put visions into their heads, without learning to discontent their minds, without the carping rights of a wedded wife and her legitimate child, they were near perfect for Old Sir, and he for them.

But a finger was jabbed into the still waters of their serenity, and it was the pointing finger of God. It followed the ebony woman everywhere, and there was no ignoring what it meant: repent. The ebony woman went down on her knees and prayed for mercy on her soul. She spent the night in a pool of tears. By dawn her prayers reached heaven's heights, and the pointing finger disappeared. She rose up, shouting, "I been redeemed. By the blood of the Lawd, I been redeemed." From that day forth, she sinned no more. From that day forth her thighs were sealed.

She let Old Sir be her boarder. It was not a fair exchange, but it was better than banishment. They sat at the table together, an act more equalizing than any they had ever performed in bed. He came twice a day for his meals, and she fed him so well that he wanted to sleep more than anything else. He took to nodding in his chair, his hands clasping his contented paunch. Whenever he opened his eyes, she was there, moving quietly, humming softly, that classic face floating above him like an ebony carving. She had been his since she was fifteen. She had given him the last child of his loins. She had loved him, and now she cherished him. Who was to say one was less than the other? Her sweetness strengthened Old Sir. When he fell sick, she put him into her bed and tended him until he felt well, and she and the butternut child made do on a quilt by the fireplace, her hand hauling back to smack the girl if she complained that the floor was too hard.

As Old Sir grew older and his empty jaws grew tired of trying to chew, she cooked everything to swallowing softness, and again her hand hauled back if the girl's lips pouted over her plate. As Old Sir grew careless about his clothes, she gave the butternut girl the care of them, and her hand was quick to let the girl know how good she learned to iron them. There were more of Old Sir's clothes in his woman's house than in his own, and he was cleaner when he left her house than when he came.

Then one long stretch of rainy weather, with all his going back and forth, Old Sir came down with a powerful cold in his chest. The ebony woman put him to bed and bedded down on the floor beside him. She would have been warmer by the fireplace, but Old Sir was burning up with fever and tossing off the bedclothes, and she wanted to stay close by to keep him covered.

The cold she caught from him was worse than the one she cured him of (and the cold she caught from the bedroom floor would have been bad enough by itself). And forcing herself to stay on her feet was more than one pair of lungs could bear. She died spitting blood. Old Sir had a box made, and he and the butternut girl, now grown to a near woman, put a couple of shovels in a wagon and carted her off to the place in colored town where the colored folks dug holes for their dead. Old Sir read a few words out from the family Bible: "Intreat me not to leave thee, or to return from following after thee: for whither thou goest, I will go; and where thou lodgest, I will lodge: thy people shall be my people, and thy God my God: where thou diest, will I die, and there will I be buried: the Lord do so to me, and more also, if ought but death part thee and me."

The butternut girl went home to clean up and air out like her mother did after sickness. In a way, doing so was a memorial to her mother. But Old Sir had nowhere he wanted to go, not to the big house with one old broken-down servant boy as doddery as himself, and not back to the little house where what had once been would never be again.

So he laid himself down on his ebony woman's grave. And no one said yea, and no one said nay, because colored folks know better than to tell white folks what to do and what not to do. He lay there three days and three nights. The morning of the first night he was too sick with double pneumonia to move if he had wanted to. By the second night he was no longer really conscious of his suffering. On the third day he was in a coma, and sometime during the third night he died.

The colored folks went and told Young Sir like it was something they had just discovered, like they didn't know how Old Sir got there, or what he was doing lying cold dead on a colored grave. They acted like they didn't know nothing, because they knew that Old Sir's son didn't want to know anything either.

The butternut girl made her living by taking in washing. At first she felt shy going to where the white folks lived and tumbling around to find their back doors and inquiring of some looming shape if she had a wash for her to take home. She brought along one of Old Sir's shirts beautifully folded in the basket on her arm to show the quality of her work, and her own persuasive appearance underscored her excellence. In not too long a time she was earning enough from her several families to keep herself and her house on their accustomed course.

She missed her mother and Old Sir, but she didn't know

any better than to stay to herself. She accepted the loneliness that plagued her at day's end as her daily portion of bitter blood. She had never had a child to play with or to grow up with, and there was no remembered joy to turn her empty heart toward someone her own age. The young colored people kept their distance. Like mother, like daughter, was what they thought. They didn't want to be shot in their britches by some white man who had seen her first.

Preacher's arrival was pure providence. What he didn't know didn't scare his behind. He was just passing through town, looking for a colored face to charm with his own, when he saw the butternut woman walking straight and tall. She was on her way home from her white folks, with her big laundry basket riding on her head in perfect balance. She looked so clean and starched and she smelled so good of soap that it was a pleasure for Preacher to hitch along and smell her. There weren't any little ones peeping around her skirts, so he spoke up boldly to ask if she had a husband heading home from work. When she told him that she lived alone, he took her basket and tucked it under one great arm and asked if there were some wood he could chop or some fixin' she could find him to do in return for his supper and a beddown in the shed.

He showed her his Bible book, not to pretend he was a reading man but to show his good intent and his claim to a calling. He said he had come across seven counties, looking for the land that would speak his name. He said this land had a sweetness to it. He could feel a lingering in his feet. He asked if she knew where a clear river ran, for tomorrow he was going to tell it through colored land that Sunday was singing and shouting day. Let the burdened bring their weary loads to the riverside and comfort the fevers and frets of their souls with the blessed balm of being baptized.

They reached the road and the house came in sight, a complete house, with real clapboards instead of any old wood, a slanting roof to nuzzle off the rain, a door that wasn't hanging loose for field mice, a porch that wasn't just a step up and a stoop, not a window with a pane busted out, and curtains at each one as starched and pretty as Sunday dresses.

Preacher picked up his feet and led the way. Without a moment's hesitation he entered the place and the moment in time that would mark the beginning of the Coles family line. They were a strange mix, maybe, one a self-appointed preacher and the other a washerwoman, one with a father he barely knew, the other with a father she called Old Sir. Both were illiterate and uninformed, their intelligence never having been tested, but the woman was the man's inspiration because of her cleanliness, and the man was the woman's inspiration because of his godliness. Between them, then, there was a mutual respect that gave them the right to self-respect.

The butternut woman had no shed, so she let Preacher sleep on the floor by the fireplace, though at first it seemed strange that a man should take the lowlier bed while she took the better. At the end of a week of studying each other, Preacher got out his Bible, placed the woman's hand on top of it, and laid his own on top of hers. He prayed aloud, committing their souls to God's eternal care. Then they bowed their heads in silent prayer, and when they raised them, they were man and wife.

Her time came upon her, and the butternut woman bore a son called Isaac, who survived a difficult birth and grew in rosy health and strength. After that, Preacher did not touch her in the times when she was fertile. He knew it would take everything in his power to treasure one child, to feed him, to clothe him, and somehow to school him. The butternut woman knew better than to protest. Her mother had taught her what to expect when she sulked. Besides, she was too busy cooking and cleaning and washing and ironing and keeping up with an active baby to feel anything but exhaustion by the time night came to quiet day. When her head touched the pillow, she wanted sleep more than she wanted foolishness.

The land bore crop after crop. Preacher sold his produce in the open market, selling more than all the other sellers because his voice hypnotized the buyers. He bought a pair of new shoes for the first time in his life and was delighted to find that shoes you were sized for wouldn't pinch your feet or shift around when you walked the way other people's castoffs did. He had Old Sir's shirts to wear for dress-up. They were many years old and many times mended, but they were Sunday white and suited Preacher fine. And when he stood by the riverside with his splendid hair set ablaze by the sun and his skin all aglow with it too, the white shirt made a striking contrast.

When winter came, the time of spring planting, Preacher got to wanting a mule so bad he could almost feel

that mule pulling the plow. Preacher heard a tale of an ornery mule that was owned by an ornery man, who couldn't
cuss that mule to move no matter how many licks he laid on
his back. Preacher went to see that man, and while he was
talking with a sweeting tongue his eye latched onto a boar
and a sow and a milk cow. His other bulging eye counted
critters aplenty all over the place, enough to fill every hook in
a smokehouse and every cooling stone in a well and still
leave more animals for mating than were hanging head
down. This Mr. White Trash could eat high on the hog from
now until a lifetime from now and never feel the lack of one
boar, one sow, one milk cow.

Meat took the misery out of winter. When there was
meat, a man and his wife and his child emerged into spring
with flesh on their bones instead of folds of skin. One time,
back when he was a boy, Preacher saw a squirrel emerging
into spring. Preacher had never seen a living thing so starv-
ing thin. That squirrel was too sorry to raise a stick to. He
looked like something a hundred years old. Every rib
showed as plain as if he had been skinned, his fur was as
meager as a moth-eaten mat, and there wasn't nothing uglier
than that puny face, all drawn back like a grinning dead cat.
That dumbheaded squirrel hadn't stored enough nut meat to
carry him through the winter. Or maybe the crop had been
poor pickings. The squirrel's last little bit of life was hanging
by such a frazzled thread that one more week of hibernation
would have killed him in his nest within reach of spring's
salvation.

Preacher had a penny bun in his pocket. He threw it to
the squirrel, and that old fool didn't even run with it. He sat

back on his haunches like a natural man and held that bread between his paws like he had human hands. An old dry bun couldn't grease his insides like the meat and the oil in a handful of nuts, but it was better than another inch of dying. Preacher went without bread that day. Without that bread that squirrel might not have lived to that day's end, and Preacher knew that he would live to buy a penny bun another day. He had been taught that bread unshared is bread unblessed when someone else is hungry, whether man or beast, friend or stranger. In God's eye a penny bun can match a boar and a sow and a milk cow for magnitude in giving.

The butternut woman kept a few chickens, as did every woman with any pride. Chickens were easy to care for, easy to kill. A woman without a few laying hens could never make a cake to melt in the mouth, or rush out and wring a chicken's neck for a Sunday caller. But a pig was what a man provided, if he was worth his salt. A pig put meat on the table every single day, not just on Sunday to show off for company. Wasn't any part of a pig except his grunt that wasn't good fixin', from hogshead cheese to pickled pig's feet, from hams and shoulders and spareribs and loins to fatback, crackling, and lard chitterlings.

Preacher plain made up his mind that he wasn't going to turn away without taking the worry out of winter for as many years as mammy pigs and pappy pigs made mammy and pappy baby pigs. So he spoke for the boar and the sow and the mule and the milk cow like he didn't know any better than to think that this old cracker was the Great White Father who never said no to a deserving darky, since being white had blessed him with more than he could use. Before Preacher could offer his iron back as bond he had to stand patient while this peckerwood used up a whole month's cussing to ask if Preacher was a crazy nigger who thought he was talking to a crazy white man who pulled the hairs off his ass for any nigger crazy enough to ask.

"Nassuh, Cap'n, I never seen no crazy white gen'men," Preacher said. "Dere couldn't be no crazy white gen'men, or dey wouldn't know enough to be borned white. I never seen a colored man had that much sense. All them I know was borned in colored skin. White folks is thinking while colored folks is sleeping. Nassuh, I'm talking to a sharp-thinking gen'man that knows a bargain from a bag of wind. I'm a gospel man, Cap'n, living decent with a seemly woman and raising a son to stay out of jail. I want something you got in plenty, Cap'n, I want it most bad. And I got a willing back and a willing way to give in return."

Ole peckerwood studied it out in his mind. Now, that mule might kick someone to death someday, and better that mule kill a nigger than a white man, and he studied some more how he had more pigs stirring up the cow dung for corn than there was corn in the cow dung for them to stir up, and he wasn't fixing to build a separate pew for them runtiest ones who just stood back and let the bigger ones hog all the swill in the trough. Them scrawny two there might be a tolerable trade for the heft in a nigger's hide.

As for the milk cow, there was that skittery one that made the rest of the herd run wild any time anybody let out a holler, and just as worse, she had to be milked like her tits were glass, which took more patience than a little bit. But dumb or not, she gave good milk when she didn't kick the pail over, which made her worth equal to the help he needed to put up the house for his married daughter that had to be built before another brat was born to plague his nights with its bawling. The minute that house was hammered together as far back as his farthest land, he'd set this nigger to digging him a round cellar to keep his vittles out of stealing reach of his son-in-law, who lived to eat and make wet-bottomed babies.

Building that house and digging that cellar wasn't all that Preacher was put to do. Most of it was mule-hard, and none of it was easy. He earned those animals three times over. But he learned from the peckerwood: he learned a dozen different ways of working with his hands, and he learned how to be a self-reliant man, and that knowledge was worth whatever he paid for it in time and bone tiredness.

On the way to the peckerwood's place Preacher had to pass several deserted farms, wildly aslant on their crumbling foundations. With their broken windows and smashed doors, they were wide open to the annual assault of the equinox winds. At first they were only eyesores to Preacher. Time and tempest would lay them level. But as Preacher learned how to put a house together he began to see these sagging structures as so many lengths of lumber, most of them rotted, but some of them still solid enough for reuse.

Making deliberately brief excursions before and after his working hours (not wanting to knock at a white door too early or show a colored face at a screaming door after dark), Preacher tried to trace the abandoned farms to their owners.

The bits and pieces of information he slowly accumulated finally led him to the bank, to which most of the land had reverted. Standing respectful before the bank president and seeing by the style of his face and his fine-boned hands that this was a blue-blood buckra, raised with grace and easier to make a plea to than a hard-nosed peckerwood, Preacher asked for Mr. President's permission to finish pulling down the shacks that were near enough to falling down to hurt some heedless child who strayed too close. He'd sort the wood and use the best. The rest he'd tote away, and then he'd sweep that spot so clean there wouldn't be one rusty nail for a barefoot child to die from.

When Mr. President asked him how he was going to tote that trash away, he had the answer. There was an old wagon on one of those farms, and some fixing might fix it enough to make it hold together for a spell. Only drawback was that he didn't know where he would get a horse to hitch it to. Wasn't one colored soul he knew who had one to lend him. Would be one sorry world for colored folks if there weren't good white folks to lend a hand when there was nowhere else to turn. If Mr. President knew some gen'men who would trust him with a pulling horse, wasn't nothing he wouldn't be glad to do in return.

Mr. President gave Preacher a pondering look, like he was trying to make up his mind if Preacher was starch or sugar water. After a while, he spoke. "There is a horse that is only used occasionally. You could use him any other time, provided you were willing to drive him those special times."

Preacher told him that he'd never heard of a better bargain, and he didn't bat an eye when Mr. President said that he and that horse would be driving the dead. He needed that horse more than he needed to be afraid of a dead white man through with hating, who couldn't hurt a colored man nearly as much as a live one could, one still raising hell.

Preacher came to find out that Mr. President owned the funeral establishment, the livery stable, the sawmill, and a laundry list of other things besides, which he was holding in trust for the town until such time as other men raised their level of hope and came to buy him out—if not with cash, at least with the confidence that the South could survive.

Preacher was determined to free the Coleses now and forever from the animal terms of "struggle or die," so that his son and those who came after him would eat without wolfish hunger and learn to reach for more than meat and bread. Looking back, he would reflect that driving the dead was the easiest work he did in that winter of dogged accomplishment. It was a kind of oasis after a hard-working day. The long ride behind the plodding horse to some outlying spot was rest time for him, a time to reflect and let some of his tiredness drain off. Even when he fell asleep and had to backtrack a mile or so, the dead man was still waiting. All Preacher had to do was wrap him up in a winding sheet, hoist him like a sack of meal, and haul him off to be measured for a coffin. It wasn't steady work, but it did pay; the undertaker, happy to be saved this onerous task, was only too glad to put the pieces of change in Preacher's pocket.

Preacher already knew all about living poor; now he learned first hand what it was to die poor. The poor didn't die in houses with stately doorways. They built their doors without regard to the grim detail of dying—grubbing a living was grimness enough. Nor was there space to spare for a parlor, or any fitting room for a laying out. With the door too narrow to squeeze a coffin through and the two-room house hardly big enough to eat and sleep in, let alone hold a wake in, the poor dead cracker was carted to the coffin shop. There the undertaker kept him cooling until his widow could borrow enough to buy him some burying clothes. When the worn-out man was washed and dressed and anointed, looking better dead and at peace than he had ever looked alive and worried about how to feed all his children, the undertaker placed him in a box. He put the box in a hearse behind a horse with a purple plume, and he drove him to the home of some willing kin with a door that would let a coffin in, and a parlor to set it down in, and chairs for the crying.

Preacher never got to see the crying part of it, or the church, or the cemetery, or the scattering of flowers. But even if he had, he would have preferred his part, the quiet part, just himself and a dead stranger riding down the road together, neither one burdening the other with foolish talk. The only sound in the carriage was Preacher's sweet voice singing "Swing Low, Sweet Chariot," not loud to a living sinner but soft to a newborn soul going home to heaven.

By the time of spring planting, Preacher had earned all of his farm animals, and his shelters had been stoutly built. Nothing remained but to bring his band to the land of promised plenty. The foul-minded mule was the first challenge. He talked to that mule with a mouth of molten gold, and he walked toward that sitting-down mule with his hand cupped with kindness, and he looked at that mule like a loving brother, and he led that risen-up mule to the waiting plow and the ready earth. When he came back for the milk cow she took to the rope without tugging. Fear at this journey to the unknown rippled her hide, though, and she lowed with a heavy heart. Preacher began to sing to her long-meter, like a sobbing harp.

> "Sometimes I feel like a motherless child,
> Sometimes I feel like a motherless child,
> Sometimes I feel like a motherless child,
> A long way from ho-ome,
> A long way from ho-ome."

With soft hypnotic sounds he sang that slave lament until the lonesome bleating wore away and the trembling subsided under his stroking hand. When it came time to fetch the hogs, Preacher couldn't tote them in his bosom like a lamb, so he found two hickory poles and turned those poles into a movable pen. He kept the hogs in the V of those poles with the fancy footwork of a dancing master.

Then it was done. Preacher surveyed what his winter had brought forth, and it was good. With a mule to help him plow, his planting land doubled in size and yield. The banker gave Preacher the horse; it was the least he could do. Preacher in turn could do no less than his bound duty whenever death's right to dignity was rebuffed by a narrow door. The body wagon stood ready for hitching at the back of the barn, and a bright homemade cart went to market with Preacher every morning, piled high with produce. The unhurried horse with its garlanded hat pulled it along and Preacher walked in back, singing his wares to whatever head popped out of a window at his passing. At the market, his stall was always surrounded by satisfied customers.

At breeding time, his sow produced a fine litter of plump pigs, which she neither trampled nor ate, but suckled like a proud mother until they were old enough to fatten themselves for a shorter life than their happy greed expected. Come fall slaughtering in another year there would be enough meat to store, and cuts of ham, shoulders, and lean-striped bacon for those to whom pork had never been more than a piece of fatback putting some kind of palatable taste in a pot of rice and beans or a mess of greens.

Maybe next year he would get another milk cow. God would open the way. With a mule and a horse and a wagon for hauling, he could hire himself out to whoever needed the linked strength they and he could supply. A dollar picked up here and there between preaching and planting could bulge a saving sock into the size of a cow. Then there would be milk for those infants whose mothers' breasts sagged with sickness, and for those weaned babies leaving their mother's lap whose legs should grow straight instead of bowed, and for the ailing and the old, to add to the sugar water that flavored a toothless mouth.

Preacher drew satisfaction from healing, and he often dreamed that his son would be filled with the gift of healing too. Preacher would rather die than see a son of his content with what he had, though. His son would heal, not with the laying on of hands (a gift no mortal man should make claim to), not with senseless words mumbled over some ancestral devil's brew, but with knowledge learned from learning places, schools, and books, and men, true doctor men. Just as Melisse—owning a restaurant but not content for her son to be happy staying in the kitchen—pushed and pulled Hannibal into the shape of her ambitions, so did Preacher dream of the day when a son of his would exceed his wildest expectations. With a church that made his title proper in the mouths of his flock *and* in the mouths of white men on Sunday, with a stall that made money, and a wife who earned money, and a house kept so clean that you could eat off the floor, Preacher could have felt that his son would do well if he did no worse. But instead Preacher began to save, what he could when he could, against that day when he would free his son from the stumbling block of illiteracy that made most colored tongues mute.

A preacher's son must set an example. He must walk a long road to show the fruits of his father's God-given blessing.

CHAPTER TEN

*P*reacher's wife bore him the son that he longed for, and they named him Isaac. He was a beautiful baby, bright and alert, and his development was remarkable. If some cosmic eye had been comparing Preacher's progress with that of Melisse, it might have given the advantage to the former. Isaac began walking at eleven months, unsteadily but determinedly, and he began to talk shortly thereafter, increasing his small vocabulary daily.

Before he was two he could be drawn from his play by Preacher's Bible as if it were a magnet. He sat entranced when his father made the book talk. He tried, his mind receptive and ready, but the book wouldn't put the words in his mouth. The words were too big: holyfication, revelation, glorimostest, believering. A Bible book was for preacher people like his father who could start it to sprouting whenever he opened it, whether he held it upside or down. His father's face could listen out even when the Bible book was a far piece away. By a riverbank, where he and his father sat filling their pail with fish for a fish fry, or in the deepening woods, he on his father's heels hunting a possum for supper, the words would come on the wind, whispering so softly that only his father knew the right moment to cock his ear. Then his father would tell what the words told him, with the fishes leaping up to listen or the trees bending low to hear and himself trying to catch the words in his mouth, but even one word was too much of a mouthful.

At three he asked for a book, a little bitty book. His hands outlined the size of book that would have the kind of words that a little bitty boy could fit his palate to. Preacher bought him an introductory reader, not because he knew that that was a suitable beginning but because it was the only book that matched the shape that Isaac had described. Isaac loved that book like he had given birth to it. He never let it out of his sight, as if he were waiting for it to say its first word. He carried it when he went with his mother to deliver a wash. More often than not a show-off child of the house would descend upon him while he waited for his mother to be paid and to gather up the next batch of cleaning, snatching the book from him and making it talk, knowing that this said *c* and this said *a* and this said *t* and together they said c-a-t, cat. Repeating it once was enough to latch it tightly in Isaac's mind.

By the time he was four he could spell his way through his book with only occasional pauses for breath. He had learned to make a book talk. Fine, but now he was hell-bent to acquire even more power in a place called school. He couldn't be persuaded to wait until he was six. He had to go see what school was about. It was a learning place, that much he knew, and there was nothing else he needed to know to make his mouth water. He said he could walk those five miles to and five miles back without getting lost or feeling tired. He was big for his age and no mama's boy.

Preacher prepared him for disappointment, but he could have saved his speeches. Isaac didn't know his alphabet in its orderly progression from *a* to *z*, but he knew the name of every letter. He didn't know what counting was, either, but he knew by rote every numbered page of his book. There was no symbol in that book that he couldn't recite. His mind was so clearly a sponge that the examining teacher had no conscientious choice but to admit him. She just prayed that his mother had him toilet-trained, or at least instructed to say "when."

The small academy was private, of course: the "public" in "public school" did not encompass members of Isaac's race. The teachers, though women of good education, were not trained in their field. They were Northern spinsters of means, steeped in the New England tradition of noblesse oblige and passionate in their belief that man is not sustained by bread alone, but by bread and books. With the cause of Southern people of color still close to their abolitionist hearts, they and others of their kind and conditioning set up little private schools in many rural areas. These brave women forced the issue of public education, of teaching the children who would someday be leaders of their race how to speak for themselves, articulately and with dignity. The token fee tied in the corner of Isaac's handkerchief and pinned to his shirt for safekeeping was not enough to cover what it cost for him to attend. Its purpose was to make him feel prideful, to impose an obligation to work for what his parents were paying for, to encourage perfect attendance if he really wanted his money's worth.

Isaac blossomed at the small school, and all of his hard work came to fruition his final year there, when his unrelenting instructor was a woman named Miss Amy Norton Norton—twice blessed with that revered name through the marriage of third cousins. This was to be her last year in the South, and she was determined to squeeze every ounce of potential out of her pupils. Isaac was eager to take what she had to give; he was eleven going on twelve but old for his age, and smart enough to know what was good for him. When Miss Amy Norton Norton asked him toward the end of the school year how he felt about going to school up North, he tripped on his tongue telling her how good it felt. It meant learning. It meant leaving Mama, but that hadn't bothered him at first—not because he didn't love Mama, but because he loved learning more.

Preacher took him to the train. His mother stayed home, not knowing if she could stand to let him go by himself onto that big scary machine. Miss Amy Norton Norton was up in the front of the train in the compartment where the white passengers rode, and Preacher and Isaac stood outside of the colored coach, at the edge of the moment of saying good-bye. "May the Lord watch between me and thee, while we are absent one from another," Preacher said softly. And then he put the words into a soft song, sweet and sad as chiming bells. Then the train dispatcher sang "All aboard," harsh white singing, but contagious with promise. Isaac gathered his things to step aboard, too excited to feel the wrench in his heart. Eleven years old and big for his age, he still looked a long way from grown. As he climbed into the train, Preacher's hand pressed hard into his shoulder. The loving pressure of that hand would stay with Isaac forever.

Preacher sang louder to cover his crying. Over and over he sang, "May the Lord watch between me and thee, while we are absent one from another. Go with my blessing. Go with God." Isaac's waving hand trailed out the window, and Preacher followed it with his eye until he could see only a trail of smoke.

Their parting was not unique. All over the South such sacrificial scenes were taking place, the giving of gifted colored children to the North where their mettle could be tested, their potential realized. Most of them would always be exiles. No free man returns to the yoke, but the South that was in them was in them to stay. What lingered was not the harshness of its whites, or the hovels of its blacks, but the beauty of its land, the abundance of its beauty. That remembered child, waking to the morning of the South, and rushing out to fling his arms around its rich scents, its rustling wood, its tapestry of color—that child, now man grown, spends the rest of his life pretending that he prefers the memory of some other place. For his children, yes, for his ambition, yes, for his self-respect, yes, but for his remembering there is no sweeter memory than the South.

Preacher lingered on the platform, sad but not sorrowful. His son had given him much joy, and the tears in his eyes were tears of loss, but they were also tears of pride and hope. He finally turned away from the empty tracks. He had given much of his life to the healing of souls, and now he had given up his only son so that someday he could learn how to heal with a different science.

When the train got to Washington, Miss Amy fetched Isaac, buying him a ticket for her parlor car. He brought his paper sack of food with him. He'd saved the best pickings for Miss Amy, who had got on board the train back home with no sign of a parcel that looked like food. Miss Amy thanked him for his thoughtfulness but explained that they would eat hot meals in the dining car. She gave his greasy sack to a porter to dispose of, sensing that a colored porter would prefer this delicate cover of disparagement to her telling him right out from her fancy seat in the parlor car to take her white folks trash to some poor mother in the coach.

Isaac entered the Chestnut Hill home of Miss Amy and her father as her protégé. He ate his meals with them, and learned his manners from them, and served as a servant of sorts. He slept on a separate floor with the colored servants, old retainers who were set in their duties and jealous of sharing them. They relinquished such a meager portion of chores to Isaac that it was child's play to complete them, but Miss Amy was satisfied that he was improving his character by working his way through school, if only nominally.

Miss Amy sent Isaac to the day school that her married brother had attended as a boy, convinced that his mind would rot in public school. She remained militant about the right of colored children to free education, but she believed that in Boston public schools, crowded as they were with children of Irish immigrants, the level of excellence expected would fall far beneath the high-water mark she set for Isaac.

When Isaac's spring term ended, he found himself going with Miss Amy and her father to a distant island. It was an impossibly grand adventure for a backwoods boy whose only experience of islands was as places for shipwrecks in stories. That they were going on a *vacation* made the journey even more of an unknown adventure. He knew about visits—they were trips you took to see somebody sick or bury somebody dead. But a vacation was going someplace just to be going someplace, and having a place to live in once you got there. And the place! It was a sprawling four-story affair, blue with white shutters, with a big porch for sitting; the idea that a house this size would sit empty for eight months out of the year was beyond Isaac's ken.

They had only been on the island a day when they had to take the carriage down to the dock to fetch Miss Amy's brother and his family, who had come for their annual re-union with Miss Amy's father. Miss Amy's brother had moved to California some years ago, his sensibilities never having quite adjusted to New England's aridity, nor his temperament to the prudishness of the Boston well to do. The cross-country trek with four children, trunks, pets, a nurse, a personal maid, and a wife who would have preferred to flaunt her Parisian dresses in a more fashionable locale was long, tedious, and hardly worth it, except that Miss Amy's father was old enough to change his will on a whim.

Isaac slept alone, in a bedroom on the top floor. In this

way he lived at a remove from the other children, and also in that Miss Amy made sure that he had sufficient chores to keep his character from succumbing to summer wilt. Her brother was more lax, as was his nature, and Miss Amy regretted that his brood fell outside of her jurisdiction. But Isaac ate with the other children, learned to swim with them, and spent as much time as he could riding beside them in their pony cart. Though they knew that he was colored, they were still too young to know that they should care. His copper skin was scarcely darker than their own summer-tanned faces, his manners had certainly been more strictly supervised, and his accent was well on its way to being indistinguishable from the speech he was exposed to at school and at home.

Isaac loved the island, which in the 1880s showed no advance signs of the coming century of cars and cocktail parties and colored people above the servant class. The carriages and pony carts enhanced the island's charm without really increasing its pace. City ways were left behind. Innocence walked barefoot down every dirt road. There were hay rides and boating, lawn croquet and lemonade, days spent picking in the woods when the blueberries ripened, clambakes and the fire company's band serenading the summer night. Where the Norton children went, Isaac went too, and the Norton children went everywhere, with their pony cart, their sailboat, their secret tree house, their lemonade parties (held on the glassed-in porch when it rained). Wherever they were, it was lonesome someplace else.

The strong will of many a determined New England mother was sooner or later dissolved by the sight of her deserted child scuffing the dirt in front of his door, ordered to stay behind while the rest of the lively herd went off on some adventure with the Norton children and "a boy whose ancestors ate each other." The trouble was that Isaac never showed his cannibal side. There was nothing about him to make children shy away. A little boy born with copper skin set down amid a swarm of little boys with copper skin on summer loan was almost impossible to single out unless some overcurious mother were to make the ridiculous request, "Will the real copper boy go home."

Isaac was part of it all until the year he turned fourteen. In the winter of that year Miss Amy's father died, and in the summer of that year the Norton children were taken to Europe. Their island visits were over, their father no longer bound by his own greed to make an annual pilgrimage to the keeper of the purse. There was no need, for he had won: the family textile mills were all his. With them he bought an ambassadorship. Now a member of the really rich, he wanted something outside the reach of the merely rich, who only stay rich by never touching their principal. For the really rich, who can buy anything, and have already bought it, an ambassador's title—with no cash required but the profuse spending of it implied—was life's *ne plus ultra*.

The will left Miss Amy some coupons to clip and the family houses as legacy, which was no more and no less than her spinsterhood expected. She could keep herself in comfort in the only two places where she felt at home. She wanted the familiar; her brother wanted the foreign. He wanted more, and he got it, but what is the measure of contentment?

That summer, Isaac and Miss Amy made the passage to

Martha's Vineyard as they always had. The rambling summer house felt empty, though, and somehow foreboding. Other things had changed on the island as well. Without the Norton children, and their pony cart and sailboat—both sold because neither Miss Amy nor Isaac could think of a sensible reason why a poor boy working his way through school should be saddled with their upkeep—Isaac was without the ballast that heretofore had kept him afloat in a sea of maternal misgivings. Now the island's mothers threatened dire punishment, the loss of precious privileges and worse, to any whiny gutless child who had no stomach for snubbing Isaac. There was no time to let him down lightly. He was taller by a head than he had been the previous summer, and his voice had lost its limp innocence. Over the winter this playful dog had grown wolf-sized, his nature unpredictable. The children's safe world was now imperiled, and the protective instinct of a mother compelled her to keep her charge at a distance.

A group of mothers made an afternoon call on Miss Amy. They arrived in a neighborly and friendly fashion, in accordance with the unwritten rule that summer was not officially in season until the Norton house was open and its occupants receiving. With their mouths appropriately at half mast, the mothers paid their respects to the memory of Miss Amy's dear departed father. With their mouths smiling like watermelon slices and their voices climbing over one another to outdo each other's eagerness, they trilled their pleasure at her brother's exciting rise to an equally impressive realm. Tea was poured, and they sipped it more and more slowly. No one wanted to be the first to have to start. The stones they had brought to throw at Isaac grew heavy in their hands.

A silence fell that the sipping couldn't fill. A throat was cleared, but courage faltered. Another throat started to emit a sound but changed its course to coughing. Waves of embarrassment rolled over the room. Then one red-faced woman whose pounding eardrums gave her the sensation of drowning in a terrible sea flung her stones and floated free. Stone after righteous stone was thrown until the helter-skelter pile rolled back the tide. Whoever saved herself had saved her child, her girl child, from a fate worse than drowning—a life not worth living. They saw their cause as just, and they felt they had presented it tellingly, especially since Miss Amy did not challenge it.

But Miss Amy would never have stooped to reply to the women's insults, as they should have known. If she kept quiet, it was because there was no way for her to be as sure of their daughters as she was of Isaac. When she was asked if the matter could now be considered disposed of, forgotten, she said that it could be. Relieved, and in haste to change the subject, no one thought to ask her if it would be. It would neither be forgotten nor forgiven. Miss Amy's summers on the island were already reduced, saddened by fleeting memories of other years and other children. Now these women had taken the only child Miss Amy had left and twisted him into a savage shape with their mouths.

Miss Amy saw the mothers to the door, giving no sign that she would never invite them to cross its threshold again. Nor would she cross theirs. But as the days advanced no sign was needed to spell out the obvious. The mothers dismissed their worries, deciding that Miss Amy's retreat from their tea tables was due to her delicate concern that her mourning dress might cast a pall over their parlors. They kept in touch by sending over broths and custards accompanied by calling cards inscribed with the hope that she was feeling better, though no one had it from any authority that she was feeling ill.

Isaac accepted his separation from the camaraderie of summer with the stoicism that was part of his school's curriculum, and part of a colored child's nature. He learned to live inside himself earlier than other people do (and some people never do). He learned to count his blessings and take everything else in stride. The premature end of his childhood illusions did have one very sweet compensation, though: every Friday he was allowed to take Miss Amy for an afternoon drive in her elegant little phaeton. His hand promptly became adept at holding the reins of her beautiful, spirited, fast-stepping bay. It was a bigger summer bonus than jogging about in a slowpoke pony cart that couldn't go half the places that a real horse and carriage could go with ease and get there twice as quickly, and Miss Amy knew it. She rode beside him, not telling him what to do because she saw that he knew.

Perhaps some cosmic force saw and approved the parallel paths two horses trotted down: Isaac, with his beloved Miss Amy at his side, and Hannibal, with Gram at his back. The hack Melisse had hired perhaps rattled along a bit more unsteadily than Miss Amy's phaeton, and Gram's stories to Josephine of the golden days of her childhood that Hannibal soaked in were touched with a sadness whose depth Miss

Amy's tales never approached. And Miss Amy did not embellish her accounts, except as the remembering eye adds height and breadth to everything. Miss Amy rode in a smooth continuum of time never torn from the calendar by war. Her way of life would die of natural causes; she would not even live to see it. Gram's way of life, though, had been cut down in its bloom. The flower of the South had rotted in the slime of slavery, the root no substance to the stalk, and the stalk suddenly obscenely ejaculating until it lay limp and self-abused in a burial of petals. Gram had pressed those petals between the papers of her memory before they could be swept away by the winds of war that sucked up everything else.

And so as Isaac sat beside Miss Amy, the gifted and the giver, Hannibal sat in his separated seat, coachman to Miss Caroline. Yet Gram, without lifting a finger except to point to the spot where Hannibal was to serve the ladies their picnic lunch, without contributing a dime or being disposed to let so much as a penny go to waste on Hannibal's potential, without one kind word of encouragement or advice, Gram was in her way as inspiring to Hannibal as Miss Amy was to Isaac. Isaac became what Miss Amy had foreseen; Hannibal became what Gram had to see to believe.

Occasionally Miss Amy let Isaac have free rein with the carriage, and when she did he drove them far and wide. He sensed that after this summer he would never come again to this jewel of the Atlantic, though he never dared question Miss Amy regarding the future, nor did she volunteer any information. If this was to have been the summer of his unrestrained passion, it was the island that received it. No woman would ever have as many facets for him as its sea, as many surprises and treasures as its highlands and lowlands, as much enduring beauty, as much quiet grace. His capacity for love, made to seem brutish and shameful by Miss Amy's neighbors, could now never surrender its self-control to lower levels of fulfillment. When he was ready for a wife, he might feel for her in the hide of his body, but in the New England overlay of his mind he would never admit to her existence. His tryst with the island, in the summer he came into puberty, was one of the few romantic adventures of which he would have total and tender recall in the winter of old age when forgetfulness torments the day and only the unforgettable orients the mind.

At summer's end Isaac packed his clothes and his boy's belongings for the trip back to Boston. This time he left no token behind as he had in other years, in company with the other children who firmly believed they were leaving a talisman to ensure their return. He was through with childish acts and childish hopes. Next summer he would be fifteen, old enough to stay alone in the city, and big enough, if he kept growing, to get a man's job and a man's pay. He had watched the red-capped porters in busy South Station on his way to and from the island—middle-aged men for the most part, their backs bent, their faces bubbling with sweat, on a treadmill trot on tired flat feet.

In this heyday of the railroad's prosperity, with motor-cars and airplanes scarcely dreamed of, the parlor cars were the mobile drawing rooms of the rich, and the black men who served them as waiters or porters or redcaps received extravagant tips for their coldly calculated servilities. All of their bowing and scraping was directed toward an end that justified the means. They saved their tips, and sent their sons to high school; they saved their tips, and started little businesses. Though generations to come might gloss over these beginnings, this was the beginning of the colored middle class. In Isaac's hometown the tiny station had been a way stop, with one train passing a day that nobody got off of and only a few ragged colored people heading North got on, and redcaps with extended palms were unnecessary and unknown. In South Station, though, a smart-stepping boy could earn himself enough in the summer to send himself to school in the winter. If he could stomach the servility, a man could ensure his future.

Settling down to sleep on his last night on the island—his decision made, his mind content with the fact that Miss Amy would no longer have to have him as her summer problem—Isaac did not dream a boyish dream of someday returning in triumph, world-renowned physician to presidents, kings, and ambassadors, and rich enough to have a carriage of his own drawn by two Arabian horses, in which he drove Miss Amy scornfully past all the kneeling neighbors who beseeched him for cures. And maybe he would open his doctor's bag for them, and maybe he wouldn't. He did not dream this dream of fame and riches. Even in his subconscious he served no other god but Asclepius, and Asclepius was a jealous god, even more so than immortal Mammon.

There had never been any question, any doubt, about Isaac's becoming a doctor. Preacher had made God a vow, and the moment Isaac leaped from his mother's mutilated womb, a man-child strong in limb and lung, he was hostage to that vow. Preacher carried in his mouth the pearl of Christ, and he passed it on to Isaac, and with it a compassion which never corrupted itself by sifting among the sick for the heaviest purse. Even at this young age, Isaac looked on medicine as a personal challenge. He had seen the puny die and the strong live. As a child in the South he had known children too sickly to play, too sickly to know that life offered nothing better than the joy of living. He was made for this life, and not just because Preacher had breathed it into him from his first days of understanding. There was the time during his adolescence when he had held a small trembling bird in the power of his hand and watched as it flew high and far away, its broken wing mended and its trembling halted—able to fend for itself once more as a result of his care. From this, Isaac learned the power of his hands, and he also learned that to be whole was to have a chance.

Isaac did not plan to grow rich. The idea that his descendants would come to take summer vacations on Miss Amy's island along with others of their kind, that they would stay in the same houses and ride in cars that cost more than carriages, that they would sip expensive spirits of an idle afternoon on a front porch while a colored woman stood over a stove in the kitchen, perfectly amenable to serving her own kind, was beyond his most absurd fantasy. When Isaac entered medicine, cars hadn't yet been invented, cocktails hadn't yet been invented, and the idea of colored people taking vacations had not yet been invented either. Isaac naturally felt that his descendants were destined for a fate superior to that of anyone else's descendants, but the sight of them sleeping in Miss Amy's master bedroom and throwing out some of her things because they didn't match the standard set by the house's newer furnishings would have made him rub his eyes, hard.

CHAPTER ELEVEN

*T*he central irony of Isaac's life might have been that all of the material comfort he would obtain had less to do with his own (unimpeachable) toil than it did with the emotional emptiness of his marriage.

Isaac's diligence paid off with a scholarship to Harvard. That he was a social outcast there did not surprise him at all; he did not want to be liked, just respected. The only way for a colored man to be respected at Harvard was to consistently receive higher marks than his classmates, and he did. From birth Isaac had known himself to be the receptacle for other people's hopes that went far beyond thoughts of his individual happiness. He was a flag bearer of sorts, and he knew it, and he knew, just as others before him knew, that too many people would take enjoyment from his failure for him to consider for a moment deviating from his course.

Preacher and his wife did not live to see their son graduate from medical school, but Isaac sensed that somewhere, somehow, they were with him. He felt their presence again the day he opened his first practice in New York. He was soon overwhelmed: many doctors compete to minister to the needs of the wealthy few, but doctors willing to treat patients with little money soon find they have more patients than they know what to do with. He lived in a garret on the top floor of a handsome brownstone on Strivers' Row, let to him by a sympathetic colleague. That same colleague hounded him daily about the sorry state of his love life. Didn't Isaac know that a wife was part of a doctor's equipment, that a "family doctor" inspired more confidence when he was also a "family man"?

For a long time Isaac shrugged off his friend's badgering. The prospect of a wife to bed and board was never one he had found attractive, and if he harbored any baser needs he had long ago learned to keep them to himself. But finally the day came when he relented enough to take time out from his evening to have dinner with a young woman his colleague knew, a schoolteacher, fair skinned, graceful, and from an unimpeachable family. Soon enough they were married. There were too many advantages: marriage gave a busy doctor a home where he could get a meal without waiting for a table and a wife to mend his shirts, keep his social life in order, and give him sons to carry on his name.

For her part the schoolteacher had married for love, or at least it had seemed to her that a schoolteacher—the pinnacle of professions for a woman of her race and time—could not help but fall in love with a doctor, an even higher peak in her race's progress, and one who was Harvard, handsome, and fair skinned. He seemed a perfect choice for a husband, and if wedding vows did not lead immediately to the sort of passion she had been led to expect, perhaps that would come in good time. As a schoolteacher, she had accustomed herself to observing all of the rules of morality. As a doctor's wife, she was also expected to be immune to temptation. Marriage made sex permissible, desirable, but marriage bound her to one partner, a man whose time of love was contracted by work to some hasty unfinished hour in a bed too late come to and too soon left. The disordered bed of a fever-ridden patient, with her high-pitched cries, her flashing eyes, and her flesh like fire, would not release him to the fevers of the schoolteacher, who would not die if unattended.

But she was a woman of dignity, who would be too faithful to her home and children to let her unused nights diminish the meaning of her days. She deployed her energies a dozen ways, so that her mind wouldn't defile her or her body betray her to the seducers of other men's wives. When she could no longer deny that their relationship was hollow as a reed, she still preferred a public appearance on the arm of a doctor to a private, secret place where love could lie beside her. Her skin would still become flushed with pride at being Mrs. Dr. Coles, and when it did she did not look like a neglected woman. Her trembling was imperceptible. Since she did not look rejected, she supposed she did not feel rejected; she had so much that was more impressive than the thing that no nice woman ever talked about.

The children she gave Isaac grew older, making friendships, riding bicycles, less at her heels in her free hours home from school. The young sleep-in who took charge of them in their mother's working hours was also much less at their beck and call. She was left to do more housework, conscientiously turning herself into the Coleses' housekeeper so that Mrs. Dr. Coles would be able to sit with a book on her lap when she came home from school after a long day of trying to put a smattering of hygiene and an intelligent tongue into newly arrived Southern heads. The schoolteacher began to feel like a fifth wheel. Her home was taken care of, and her children were taking care of themselves. Her husband's few requests were directed toward the willing little servant. The outlets for her femininity that the schoolteacher had been raised to expect from marriage were being closed off to her one by one.

She could have felt sorry for herself or she could have come to terms with it, and she chose to come to terms with it. With quiet objectivity, she began to adapt her instincts to another image. Slowly, with much stopping and starting and grinding of gears, her masculine genes began to function and gave her life a new direction, and made money her standard of success.

She began to buy slum property, one piece at a time, then two, then three, and in time a whole row of ramshackle multiple dwellings. Most of them had been foreclosed, and she bought them for a song, often just for the unpaid taxes. To the previous owners, disinterested inheritors, the cost of the extensive repairs necessary to make the flats livable would mean years before there was any profit in their profits.

The schoolteacher's profits were almost immediate, though. She did not improve her properties. She did not have to, for she never had a vacancy. There was a war on, and work for everybody. Blacks were coming in droves from the South, and no decent neighborhood would have them. They did not even go there to look. They looked for the familiar, the run-down streets, the ragged houses.

They asked for no more than a room at cheap rent. This the schoolteacher gave them, in addition to inside toilets and tap water. If the hall toilets were often choked and unusable, they were still used, for they were a step up from an outhouse buzzing with greenflies. Though the water ran red from rusty pipes and couldn't be drunk until the rust settled, it saved an old woman a lot of walking to and from a spring way yonder with a heavy pail. If the ceilings were unsightly, and sometimes a piece of plaster fell, if here and there a floor board was chinked up with rags to keep out the rats, if the roof leaked on top-floor tenants so badly that their rooms were crowded with basins, so be it. It was still a lot better than the hanging tree.

They were up North. No more lynching rope. No more burning crosses. No more walking in the gutter to let "Mr. Charlie" have the whole sidewalk. No more "Aunties," no more "Uncles." No more dying for want of a doctor, no more children working in the fields who didn't know their asses from their elbows while the school bell rang for the white man's child. Up North, a man could learn that reading and writing wouldn't hurt anybody. A woman could learn to hope for more than she had. If they lived near the railroad tracks and the Northern air was heavy with smoke and grime, still it filled their lungs with freedom. No hardship would drive them away. The indescribable beauty of the South would haunt them forever, though, would make the babbling old beg to go home to die, would make the young wish they could have it both ways when a measure of prosperity came.

The schoolteacher never had any vacancies. All the money that came in never had to go out. When a minor accident occurred—a step collapsed, and a tenant turned his ankle—she was prompt to replace the step and offer her apologies. She collected outgrown children's clothes and toys for Christmas distribution. She never evicted a tenant who was between jobs, even occasionally lending him money at an interest rate much lower than a usurer would have demanded to help tide him over. Every month she would ride the trolley to the bank, her money bag full of collected rent. When she stopped in on her tenants to make her hated monthly call, she could never help being bemused by the fact that Isaac may have been at a particular apartment the night before. The door would certainly have been flung open more eagerly for him than for her, his doctor's bag eyed with reverence for the medicine it contained and their mouths poised for excuses for use when he requested payment upon leaving. These were people who lived at the lowest level. Food came first for them, rent came next, shoes for the children came when they could, and the doctor came when he was called.

The schoolteacher grew money-rich with each influx from the South, but Isaac was only enriched with charity, a crazy commodity to peddle for cash. He worked to the danger point of tiredness trying to keep migrants alive in their harsh adjustment to freedom's hunger, to the numbing cold that crippled the limbs of the old, to the wet, pneumonia-riddled cold that filled the funeral parlors with fragile children in cheap caskets, to the city smoke that filled lungs not used to it and laced the lips with blood, to the epidemics that raced like wild horses, leaving no house without its wailing, to the pavements that could not be plowed and planted with purging greens to pacify a belly hard as stone from winter's coarse and costive diet.

Against all odds, and all of Isaac's modest expectations, the grim tide of disease and death slowly diminished under his vigilance. He was never surer of his reason for living, or of his indifference to dying. As long as he could save more lives than the one he was losing in a steady drain of stamina, he was content. From among those saved might come the great man, or the father or forefather of the great man, the man made for his time, the man that history would mark.

The doctor saved enough ghetto lives to keep the schoolteacher's supply of employable tenants at a constant level. They were humbly grateful for her forbearance in letting them have a roof to be sick under, and while they owed the doctor their lives, a debt they could never repay, the back rent they owed the schoolteacher could be reckoned in dollars and cents. In a few years the schoolteacher had more money than anybody she knew. And everybody she knew wanted to help her spend it. She could not avoid the obligations that money brought. Though little interested in socializing, she had to give parties to showcase her affluence.

Her parties were serviced by the best caterers, whose

unhappy white waiters walked through the crowds with thinly veiled disdain. There was imported champagne, which uninstructed tongues lapped like water because it did not kick like a mule or clobber them until the morning after. The schoolteacher grew tired of spending her money on other people's hangovers, but her exciting parties—in such contrast to her sober inclinations—had become an institution. Her friends, for whom she had real affection despite her impatience for their drunken performances, looked forward like children to the major holidays and the hospitality that she alone could provide.

She did not deny that she alone had the means to celebrate a holiday without robbing Peter to pay Paul. But she soon devised a way to do the same with more élan and without any means at all. Her Sunday reading had come to include the society papers of the metropolitan newspaper, not because she cared a whit what white society did, but because she did not want to do it differently, since some of her guests were in the employ of these seasoned socialites and knew how things should be done. In her reading, she made the discovery that in the case of an invitational charity ball an admittance fee was perfectly in order, the accepted custom being to deduct expenses from the proceeds and donate the rest to some worthy cause. This was perfect: between the half-clothed children in the ghetto where she taught school (her own sons were resident students at their father's prep school in New England), and her renters, who raised their families on less than a living wage, she knew off the top of her head more than enough deserving names to fill the pages of the poor. Where before she had felt only irritation at the time consumed in planning a party, organizing a charity ball gave her a feeling of purpose, an expectation that the end would justify the effort.

She was smart enough to form a committee of congenial friends. Though it was she who paid whatever bills came due in advance of the ball, and she who would have to pay out of pocket whatever bills came after the ball if the door receipts were disappointing, she encouraged her committee to feel that their enthusiasm and their ideas were as important as her bankbook. Her friends responded by tripping over each other to contact people, both those they knew well and those they knew slightly. The schoolteacher had shrewdly chosen her committee for their social position: those they knew slightly were glad to come to get to know them better, and perfectly happy to pay for the entrée they had never been offered for free. In time they would be insiders too, serving on committees.

The schoolteacher chose a colored lodge for the site of her first ball, the century being too new for even a passing glance at a ballroom in a white hotel. But she and her committee transformed the bleak hall with flowers and floating streamers and soft lights, and a lot of soap and water. The evening was a smash. It was the biggest event in the short and lively history of colored society in New York. No one with a dollar to spare or a dress to wear had stayed away. The money raised exceeded all estimates, and it would do so much good in so many areas of painful need—for babies sleeping in bureau drawers, older children sleeping in bags on a dusty floor, school-aged children without shoes, cripples without crutches, and eyes half blind without glasses. So many needed so much that once the schoolteacher started helping a little she became overwhelmed by how much more she could never hope to do. She saw a dead man lying shamed in an old patched shirt—and God knows a man should lie down for the last time in a new white shirt. She saw the old held together with string that once was bone, their shriveled, hunger-hardened stomachs wanting no more than a pinch of snuff tobacco. It was little enough, but it made all the difference in the hours of a man's drawn-out dying.

The successive balls were as triumphant as the first. The second ball blazed across the Christmas holidays. One inspired social climber who kept an artful eye on the mighty committee should a vacancy occur announced herself as a "patron" of the ball, a title which included the right to pin a slip of paper on her bosom with her name and rank, and the privilege of paying more to grace the dance floor than the ladies whose bosoms were unpapered. With other social climbers scrambling to follow suit, the yield was like the proverbial loaves and fishes.

The spring spectacular, blessed with springlike weather, brought contingents from Boston and Washington, the cities that considered themselves and New York a holy trinity in which New York placed a definite third. Boston was inclined to boast that none of its forebears had ever been slaves, and Washington felt a right to boast that all its best people were fair-skinned descendants of congressmen and senators, while New York could not really substantiate either claim.

Perhaps by way of maid to mistress, the schoolteacher's estimable philanthropic efforts became known to a long-established white social agency. This agency's broader aims were meeting a baffling resistance from the newly transplanted colored people it sought to help; to them a white interrogation, however sympathetic, implied a threat that they would be sent back to the South if they could not support themselves in the North. The schoolteacher was invited to a board meeting, where she sipped tea with self-consciously solicitous ladies with high bosoms and long sleeves. The meeting had been called and the schoolteacher summoned in order for the board to score her on appearance and deportment. With a score of B or more she would be offered membership, the first colored woman ever to be so honored, thereby giving the board the Christian feeling of handpicked brotherhood.

When the schoolteacher heard that she had passed muster, she was properly impressed by the honor. It was another colored first, and the curious American custom of keeping a scorecard of colored firsts was well established. She wrote the board a gracious letter of thanks, restraining the impulse to be profuse. Her careful wording acknowledged their natural right to expect an excellence in her above and beyond the requirements of equality.

Before her letter of acceptance, the schoolteacher's pity for the poor had never disturbed her sleep. When she sat on their shabby chairs (hoping that nothing was crawling around on her collar) and watched them count out part of their rent in slow little piles of nickels and pennies, she pitied them their hard times that made them a few nickels shy of the amount due, and she forgave them and, having forgiven them, she forgot them on her way to the bank.

Her balls had been inspired by her discovery that she could charge admission in the name of charity. The proceeds had been given to the ghetto poor because the genteel poor would not sell their pride at any price. All she knew about the ghetto poor was that she did not have the same grace or gentility that made poverty less obvious, less of an odor. She set about to learn more.

The agency's workers had learned very little. Their efforts to understand the day-to-day life of the swelling ranks of the urban poor had proved a dismal failure. The school-teacher could not afford to fail, though; she had a moral obligation to succeed. She was on trial before an all-white jury, whose decision would influence other decisions in other fields that colored people of ability hoped to enter. At home, at her desk, she laid out the rough beginnings of a plan. She began to think of her tenants in an entirely different light: as research material. She bought a brand-new notebook to carry into the field, and she intended to fill it with unsentimental facts. She did not for a moment identify with the people of the ghetto, any more than she identified with their common ancestors in Africa.

On her first day she was filled with confidence as she entered into the darkness of despair. She sat on the suspect chairs and invited the tenants to sit down with her. They had never sat down with her before unless they had been too sick to stand, whether she came as their rent collector or their Lady Bountiful. In either case they had always felt too poor in her presence even to act polite, too cowed by her prosperity to offer her a cup of water, which shamed their country manners since a cup of God's water was the first thing you fetched anyone, friend or stranger, who had come from a distance and whose throat might be dry.

The schoolteacher did not sit on the edge of her chair. She sat back and unbuttoned her coat to put the tenants at ease. Her hosts impaled her with astonished eyes, and her face flushed a little under the intensity of the gaze. They were almost inclined to offer her a cup of water to cool her off, but they felt she was too high-toned to cool off. A glass was more her style, but they didn't own one. An old cup could do as well in a baby's wobbly hand or a grandmother's. A glass could break the day you bought it, taking away the five cents that might have gone to a loaf of bread. They saw neither her money bag nor her charity box, so they knew she had come not to take what they were bound to give nor to give what they were bound to take but for some unhurried purpose that required their taking part in the encounter with more than dumb obedience.

Opening her notebook, the schoolteacher tapped its pages with her pencil to indicate that one was party to the other. She scanned the faces as if she were looking at an ungraded class and was resigned to letting their limping tongues take the time and a half they would need to spell out their simplistic thoughts with the ramshackle machinery of their minds. She began with the easiest questions, nodding encouragement when the answers came. She wrote them down, her pencil gliding powerfully over the paper. She was listening to their lives, and putting her listening into a visiting book as if it was worth the wearying effort to write it. Their burdened hearts began to stir from the bowels of despair. Nobody knew the trouble they'd seen, nobody knew but Jesus. And now a comforter had come to ease the crushing load of nobody knowing.

The words poured out of them, faster than her pencil could keep track, faster than her questions could fit in, sounding at first like another language, the accent so mush-mouth Southern, the English so inverted, the idiom so full of gospel images and the whole interwoven with Gullah from a grandmother's grandmother's remembering, singing, soaring African words as beautiful as African birds. And their unknown words and phrases, both Gullah and jargon, began to relate to those whose meaning was clearer. Her ear accustomed itself to the slurred speech and separated it into sentences. She understood, and her understanding sifted through the layers of her self-defenses, and the loneliness that links the deprived whatever their pearls of accomplishment became the bond between her area of need and theirs. She listened long and she listened deep, and her involvement, the full measure of her penetration, became complete.

She did not leave until a late hour, and then only because she was sick from exhaustion. Her tiredness stirred in her stomach like nausea. Her spirit was unflagged but her flesh had no feeling; she had remained seated in one cramped spot long past the point of pain. Once she had asked for water and gulped it gratefully from a cup, which if she thought about it at all she thought easier to hold in her trembling hand than water in a slippery glass.

She lost count of the people who crowded into the increasingly fetid and airless room as the glad tidings spread all over the tenement that the Listener had come. No one wanted to wait until tomorrow or any other put-off time.

They did not want her to give it all away before they got some. She was giving out hope and they did not want another day to end without it.

The schoolteacher was hungry when she reached home, and her grumbling house girl had kept her dinner hot for her, but when she tried to eat, her mouth turned to dust. She had seen too many children with bowed legs and soft bones in one day. She tried to stir her tea, but her hand could not hold the spoon on its course. With both hands, she lifted the cup to her lips, unable to wait for it to cool. She took a deep steadying sip, and the rising steam invaded her eyes, her nasal passages. Her nose felt moist, and she mopped it; her eyes began to fill, and she dabbed at them. She felt an agitation in her chest like bubbles in a butter churn. Her breath came in little gasps.

The cup was no easier to hold than the spoon. She set it down, and the tea sloshed onto her trembling hand, scalding her. For a moment, she wondered if she had been burned internally, too—she could not understand what was happening inside her. It was another moment or two before she fully realized that the upheaval inside her was a gathering storm of tears. The first few drops burned her cheeks, and then she was crying, truly crying, an act of contrition she had not performed for years.

She left the table and went upstairs, fumbling blindly along the banister. Behind the closed door of her bedroom she undressed and got into her nightgown, too dazed to perform her usual post-tenement inspection for clinging ghetto filth. She sat on the edge of the bed, shaking her long hair free and twisting it into a braid. Most women don't realize it, but their hair is part of their nervous systems, and the schoolteacher was no different. She let the long knotted rope of hair hang over her breast, too indifferent to lift it over her shoulder and let it hang down her back in its nightly place of rest. She stared at the Anglican cross on the far wall, as stark and unadorned as the cross of the crucifixion. In the quiet light from a single shaded lamp it seemed to be held in the air by the luminosity of its polished wood.

Her priest had presented it to her as a token of the many years she had devoted to Episcopalian piety. It was she who saw to the altar flowers, she who sent her girl to help at church suppers, she who gave a stained-glass window in her mother's name in the hope that it would help her Baptist soul move over to the Episcopalian side of heaven. There was never an appeal to which she failed to subscribe. She gave a double measure of her time and money. There was never a day on which she did not serve the church in some capacity, not for her soul alone but for Isaac's as well. In truth, it was his state of grace she worried about more than her own.

She could not remember when Isaac had received the sacrament. He never took time to kneel at God's altar. Sometimes she wondered if he, like many men, was an agnostic, who looked to science as his religion, or if, like many ministers' sons, he was in rebellion from the discipline religion represented. She had tried, Lord knew, to keep enough faith for both of them. The keeping of her husband's conscience was her duty as a wife. But now, after the day she had had, she did not know but that Isaac had a fundamental faith that was stronger than hers. In a book of the Bible someone had said, "Thou hast faith and I have works. Show me thy faith without thy works, and I will show thee my faith by my works." Had Isaac practiced his unorthodox religion in the alleys of the poor while hers had felt more at home in the magnificence of her church? Its magnificent structure was the first owned by colored people in the country, a century-old baroque reminder of the worldly success of its founders. The communicants, proud of their acquisition and the price they had paid for it (it being the custom of New Yorkers to boast where others might bewail), were so deep in church-building debt that their treasury could allocate no portion of its resources to the poor.

Out of the entire congregation, only the schoolteacher had done in some measure what needed to be done, the deed accomplished with the doer's heart uncommitted, the gift delivered with the giver at arm's length. From biblical wisdom had come the words "Though I speak with the tongues of men and of angels, and have not charity, I am become as sounding brass. . . . And though I have . . . all knowledge, and have not charity, I am nothing. And though I bestow all my goods to feed the poor . . . and have not charity, it proveth me nothing. Charity suffereth long, and is kind . . . beareth all things." Charity was involvement. Through another shower of tears, the cross seemed to radiate spears of shimmering light, like spokes from God's center to the center of her consciousness. For the first time in her religious life, she experienced a moment of oneness—which Preacher would have called a revelation—with God, a moment in which the spirit rewards the flesh.

On his way past her room, Isaac heard the sound of

sobbing. In the quiet night the sound was as a cry for help. Still, he knew his wife was not weeping to be heard. Her pride had never permitted her to stoop to self-pity. He could only imagine that she was ill or in pain, and he felt a prickle of remorse because he couldn't remember how she had looked that morning or when he had looked at her and really seen her. He knocked at her door. The crying cut off as if she had suddenly slit her windpipe, preferring to be caught dead than to be caught crying. He knocked again.

"Yes?" she said in a voice he didn't recognize. He was aware that her response was not an invitation, but he opened the door, the professional man concerned where the husband he wasn't might have shied away from the sound of her private sorrow. He saw her seated on the side of the bed, the covers folded back, her robe across them. It had been a long time since he had come into her room at a late hour, delicacy restraining him from disappointing her with matters unrelated to the marriage bed.

"Are you ill?" he asked from the doorway, a little embarrassed that he felt he must explain at once the reason for his intrusion lest she misunderstand. She brushed her tears away roughly with the back of her hand. "Are you ill?" he asked again diffidently from the doorway. His stubborn feet would take him no farther into her room until he had her assurance that she was in need of his medical ministrations and nothing more.

At the sight of Isaac's discomfort, the schoolteacher grimaced with embarrassment. She was mortified by the idea that he might have misinterpreted her tears as cries for love.

"There's nothing wrong," she said, her shaky voice giving lie to her words. "I've had a rough day and I'm keyed up. I'll calm down."

"Telling me might help you unwind."

"You're too tired to listen. You look tired to death. Go on to bed, I'll be all right."

"Take a deep breath." She did. "Fine . . . take another." He watched her breasts rise and subside in a broken rhythm . . . rise and subside . . . rise and subside, in a mesmerizing cadence that tied the blood in knots in his temples.

She held out her hands to show him they were quieter. He thought it was a gesture of appeal. He lashed himself for making her beg him to come to her bedside, a simple duty he would have performed without pause if she were a ghetto woman in a gamy gown, sprawled in smelly anguish on a bed unchanged all winter. What perversity made him stop short at the door of a schoolteacher? What other man would have to be summoned to a bed without sickness, a wife without blemish, a beast unbound by straps and stays? Who but himself would take this time to ponder?

He stumbled across the threshold, stubbing his toe hard against the sill. The pain buckled him at the knee and he began to pitch and sway, not from the pain so much as the monumental tiredness that his unhinged leg could not control. He felt like a fool, and he was sure he looked like one. A scalding wave of embarrassment drenched him in waves of sweat as debilitating as a hot bath. Undone, he caught a contagion of trembling. Even a fool could fumble a way to a woman's bed. Only an utter fool would fall apart before he reached it. He set his sights on the chair and plopped into it. It stayed under him. Fresh perspiration beaded his forehead from sheer relief at working this miracle without cracking the floor with his face.

"Now," he said, crossing his legs to use them as clamps, "when you're ready to talk I'm here to listen. I couldn't sleep with something upsetting you. It's useless to tell me to go to bed."

She saw that it was useless, and she also saw his beaded agony. He had come so far and he could go no farther alone. The crushing weight of the cross he carried had drained him of endurance. Her flash of concern that he would misread her tears and her attire now seemed irrelevant. This man whose manhood was more than maleness, this doctor who served one master and no mistress, was used to the night wait by the bedside of tears; he had seen grief. Nothing about her seduced him.

He smiled at her. She was as startled by that smile as if it had focused a floodlight on his face, illuminating the beauty of his bones. She had never seen him look so striking. It was a moment before she realized that she had never seen his face so defleshed, so skeletally thin that its structural perfection was as starkly emphasized as if a knife had laid him bare. A rhyme flashed across her mind, forgotten since childhood: "Beauty is but skin deep, ugly to the bone. And when beauty fades away, ugly claims its own." Her mother would sometimes recite this behind the back of some resented friend who was prettier than another woman could appreciate. But with Isaac, his beauty was embedded in his bones, which would cleave together in their symmetry until the earth's convulsions smashed them out of their sockets.

Yet that lost flesh diminished all the wealth that she had amassed. In the midst of their prosperous living, he had too often forgotten his daily bread. In the midst of the hunger that he saw everywhere on his daily rounds, bread that could not be broken into loaves for the multitudes would have been a stone in his belly. . . . She wanted to tell him that her supper had gone untasted, that she too could no longer spread her tablecloth over a coffin. But she had to tell him from the beginning.

"I spent the day in a nightmare. I watched a parade of dead souls. They had died in my houses. They had died hemorrhaging life. But others kept coming up from the South, looking to claim their piece of the promised land. My houses stayed full. My profits never fell. That property paid for itself a hundred times over. But I didn't know I was making a deal with death. I never deserved to be a doctor's wife. I wanted the label without the loneliness. You live to make live. You live with a love that mine could never match. Today, I heard your love crying in a tomb. Help me find the faith to roll the stone away. Christ the healer, help me." She began to moan, not in pain but in passion. She was in the throes of an old-time religious conversion, a convulsive surrender to Christ free of Episcopalian restraints, her naked spirit kneeling and praying for union with his.

He saw her ecstasy. He saw her wholeness, the freshness of a woman in the pink of health, a sight rarer to him than a pearl from the sea. He saw her gown, garnished with ribbon and lace, and he saw the bed turned back, a clean white bed to tempt a tired man to drink from the well of a woman without blemish. He began to undress, ripping, tearing, his clothes falling helter-skelter around him, a stubborn shoelace snapping, buttons popping. He was breathing as hard as if a sea of blood was pounding his heart against his lungs.

In the crescendo of her conversion, she witnessed the revelation, the word made flesh, Christ coming toward her in the visible body of man. If he but touched her, she would be redeemed. He thrust her down and lay beside her, his mouth against her golden mounds, his hands roaming wherever there was treasure. And then he lay on top of her and took his joy with a frenzy he had never felt before, not even at first mating, not even when his younger heart could climb the peak of pleasure and make the climb again.

When it was over he rolled away from her and gave a great exhausted sigh, like a whoosh of wind in an empty bottle. He lay as still as if he had stopped breathing. She tried to lie without moving too, so that she would not disturb this sleeping rest and peace. In the few minutes before she drifted into her own sweet sleep beside him, she reflected on the day she had just lived through, and the changes it had wrought. She thought about their tenants who had nothing, and how little it would take to improve their lives so much.

She would turn those buildings into a center of hope, a settlement house surrounded by a row of renovated flats. The settlement house, her stoutest house, would have a clinic on the ground floor, a nursery on the floor above, and offices for counseling and job referrals and whatever pressing community needs space permitted. Every flat would have a bathroom, complete with toilet bowl and tub. She would tear out the unsightly hall toilet that served six families and fouled the dank and sunless air through its open door—left open when not occupied to indicate that it was free to anyone who had business to conduct inside it, including any wandering stumbling drunk off the street to frighten the wits out of some small seated child whose mother had forbidden her to latch the door. Every unkempt cellar would be cleared of its long accumulation of vermin-breeding debris. The rotting foundation would be shored up, and air cracks sealed against the winter's biting wind and the rats' bold forays. Furnaces would be installed and radiators would replace the smoky kerosene stoves whose choking fumes were the high price paid for their low yield of heat.

Falling plaster and peeling paint would be stripped, and rotted boards would be ripped out for new ones. Steps would be widened for the old to climb more easily. There would be light from above, electric light, a learning light whose steady illumination on a schoolbook was so much better than the feeble flame from a flickering gas jet that discouraged squinty-eyed study in favor of foolish horsing around. But cooking with gas was something else, something high on her list. A gas range was clean and predictable; it made a mockery of a cussed-at, has-been ghetto coal stove with broken grates and faulty flues and holes breathing soot on everything.

For as long as possible, the rent would stay the same, and never rise higher than warranted. There would be no profits. Repairs and improvements would be a continuing process. If in time other neighborhood landlords took slow, imitative steps, then in time other neighboring tenants would make a start to a higher level of living, and an area of blight would be reclaimed. These were the bold, all-encompassing plans of salvage and salvation that she would put before the board—a settlement house (named, with their consent, for her husband), and flanking it the renovated flats for low-income families—all to be under the board's administration, all gifts outright, relinquished without strings, her own inglorious tenure ended.

For a moment she had the impulse to wake Isaac, but his sleep was too deep, too long deferred. Tidily, she put her cerebration away in the memory slot of her disciplined mind, where it would stay at the same intensity of white heat until her next meeting with the board. With a sigh of completion, she fell asleep, and the night folded down on the still spent forms of the forgiven.

It was the cold that woke her, a glacial cold like no other in her experience. She felt as if she had slept on a slab of ice. It surely must have been the coldest night in memory. The temperature must have fallen below any existing records. The city was probably at a standstill. No school bells would ring on this morning. Frozen birds must be dropping like dead flies from the eaves. The sun was shining brightly through the windows, though; she was even briefly blinded by its glare. But despite its radiance it could not budge the immovable mass of cold air, the arctic front that the weather forecast had not predicted. Still, she was grateful that the day would not have to seem more depressing for unfolding under a dark sky.

Then something struck her as odd. She shouldn't have been seeing the sky at all—the windows should have been coated with frost. Even if the sun had managed to melt them, they should have been wet and steaming, not clear and dry. Was the cold indoors? No cold felt more bone-chilling than indoor cold. Had the furnace gone out? It had never happened before, but anything could happen once. Maybe the hired man had gotten himself drunk and had forgotten to bank it for the night.

With a little moan of dismay she turned to look at her flowering cactus. Her younger son Clark had brought it home on his Christmas holiday from school. The plant was not dead. Not a petal had fallen, not a leaf had curled from the cold. Indeed, its leaves had turned toward the sun as if they could feel a warmth she could not.

Then she was struck by another curious fact. She could not relate the way she felt to any previous reaction to intensive cold she'd known. She was not shaking with it, her teeth were not chattering with it, she was not rigid with it, she wasn't knotted up in a fetal position as if seeking the womb's warmth. She was not numb at all. The feeling was indescribable.

This unparalleled cold, this cold beyond human experience, was steadily advancing up her body. Already her feet and legs were icier than she would have believed possible in a living body . . . in a living body . . . she could feel no colder if she were dead . . . if she were dead . . .

Terror struck her. Was she ill? Was she desperately ill?

Had she had a heart attack in her sleep? Had she waked to watch herself die? There was so much to do before she died. Oh, God. There was so much to undo. "Isaac!" she called, but he wouldn't rouse and there wasn't time to wait. She got out of bed and began to walk. Up and down, up and down, keeping herself alive.

The walking helped. Her heart beat evenly. She could feel the cold backing down her lower body until her feet were as warm as toast on the warm rug. As she passed the windows, the noise of the city rising up did not seem full of protesting cries. When she blew her breath against the window, it did not steam.

Her panic subsided. She wasn't dying any more than she was standing on her head. Her heart was sound—indeed, she felt wonderful, just the way she should feel the morning after a night of fulfillment. She had only been dreaming that she felt cold, only dreaming that she had called Isaac. She jumped out of bed in her sleep. She was only now really awake.

But in an inexorable moment of dawning lucidity, she knew. She was awake enough now to know that she had not dreamed any part of it.

The climax was anticlimactic. She did not scream, faint, or cry. Perhaps another's death, that incontrovertible state of nonbeing, is easier to face than the marginal moment of dying. Death is only the end of dying. She went to the bed, not to confirm the fact but to face it. When she touched her husband's stiffening hand, she drew back in a reflex of crawling flesh. She knew, or believed she knew, that the cold that had rocked her out of bed had not been the cold of outward contact but a distillation of cold, a clamor of cold sounding an alarm through her sixth sense. Out of the intensity of her physical oneness had come a mystical communication in which she had taken his dying into the warm bed of her body, not to die with him, not to die for her, but to fight for his life with the supernatural strength the resisting flesh stores for the hour before eternity.

But Isaac had died while her conscious mind was disarmed. In her waking awareness, she had leaped for her own life, running from a sleep already overslept, from a bed already robbed. In her desperate flight she had flung the covers to the foot of the bed. Isaac lay revealed in his nakedness. She drew up the sheet, smoothing it gently across his shoulders. She did not cover his face. Let the doctor draw the shroud over the dead. She could not raise her hand against him.

She must call the doctor. She would use the telephone in Isaac's room, that telephone that had rung out so many times in the middle of the night to wake Isaac with its summons.

Her hardest task would be to tell her sons. Losing a husband was a sad, hard thing, but losing a father before you're old enough to understand what that loss meant was cruelly unfair. At least she could say that she had a last night of reconciliation, however ephemeral and bittersweet. She thought of Clark, the youngest. He hardly knew his father. Would he be able to forgive him for leaving? Would he understand the reasons Isaac had for never being around much in the first place, for working himself to the bone? She would make sure that he did. That child would grow up knowing who his father was, what he stood for, what he believed in. God willing, he would follow his father's path. The schoolteacher looked down on Isaac's still body for a last time. She brushed a fingertip softly against his cold forehead, and then she turned and walked from the room.

CHAPTER TWELVE

*C*lark sat in Corinne's station wagon, waiting for the morning boat to bring another brace of Coleses to witness the barbaric rite of giving a virgin in marriage. There were other off-islanders waiting in sleek cars, and others who were just as clearly stamped "summer people" who had left their cars to walk restless pedigreed dogs or restless, radiantly healthy children. Their sun-browned holiday faces were turned seaward, waiting to catch a glimpse of the steamship, *Islander,* when she rounded the cliffs, the sun on her gleaming white flanks, her whistle sounding for a landing, the green sea parting to let her pass and quieting the waves in her wake.

Clark alone sat with a tight, tormented face, his tan

washed out by his pallor, his eye oblivious, his ears rejecting the joy around him.

The letter was like a wound in his clutched hand, its words burned into his palm, as traceable as a pattern in Braille. He had left the Oval well ahead of the ferry's arrival with the stated purpose of stopping for gas, picking up the morning paper that had come in on the early plane, and making a reservation for the ferrying of his car across the sound as soon after the wedding as space on the steamer was available.

Only the latter errand had any relation to the real intent behind his impatience to get away from the house, but he had methodically attended to them all, if only because they were too minor to find excuses for not doing them. He saved until last his major errand, which involved the post office. He did so not to postpone it or to steel himself, but because he would be incapable of concentrating on anything else once he got Rachel's letter. He would have to ask the clerk for it, having to admit his ineptitude at making three correct turns upon the post-office-box dial. Though Corinne had rented the same box year round because of its convenient height and easy-to-remember number, its summer contents were rarely addressed to Clark, and never of any interest to him, and he had never bothered to remember the combination. The telephone was a more immediate way of reaching him if a medical problem needed his attention in New York.

Rachel knew the telephone number, but she had never used it. They had an understanding. At the start of the final week of his vacation with his family, he would find an outdoor telephone booth in some section of the island far removed from the usual orbits of the people he knew and put in a call to Rachel, who knew, by prearrangement, that he would call at such-and-such an hour—or as near to that hour as possible—on such-and-such an evening, or without fail on the next night, if something unavoidable were to come up.

The call was to confirm the time and place of their departure for their two-week holiday somewhere outside the States, to a clime where the beauty of Rachel's brownness commanded extra courtesies from those who served the white-appearing American doctor and his lovely colored wife, and from those at dinner tables around or in theater seats beside them who were captivated by the harmony of their contrast, a reaction exactly the reverse of that which such a juxtaposition would have excited in their own America, the country to which they gave their love and loyalty.

It was Rachel who always selected the place where they could take their love without shame or slander. Clark had come to make a small ceremony of taking her a sheaf of travel folders on the eve of his departure for the island, to fill her time of waiting, to divert her mind from dwelling too much on the irony of his openly going to join Corinne, who had not been his wife in any real sense for years. But they both knew that he was soon to return to Rachel's constancy, slipping off behind a smoke screen of little lies that Corinne surely did not believe but accepted as her due to save face before her friends.

Last night he had talked to Rachel by telephone. He had tried to call her earlier in the week, but there had never been a free hour. A wedding in a household of women involved the father of the bride to the limit of his patience. In these final, frantic days, there were errands to run around the clock, the conclusion of the women being that they were too busy running the wedding to attend to the small-scale operations that a fairly intelligent male could execute without too many errors in judgment.

Once or twice he had been tempted to scribble a note to Rachel, just a line to say she was very much on his mind. But the gesture had seemed empty and meaningless. Why tell her what she knew already, that she was second only to his daughters in his thoughts? He had never written her anyway, not wanting to compound the secrecy of their love. Until this morning's mail, she had never composed a letter to him, not wanting him to have to destroy the tenderness that had dictated it. But now here was Rachel's handwriting, so familiar a sight on memo pads, so unfamiliar on the outside of an envelope.

When he rang Rachel the night before, it had been after midnight, and he had winced with reluctance at the thought of shattering her sleep. He knew he had sounded embarrassed about how obvious it was that he was calling her at this inconsiderate hour because he had been lured into some unavoidable commitment by Corinne.

It was true enough, though. Corinne had held a dinner party for those of her friends who had come a long way for the wedding. Not all of them had driven down, and not all of them were staying within easy walking distance of the Oval. Corinne had asked Clark to chauffeur these guests to and from her party since taxis were hard to come by, their summer demand far exceeding their limited supply.

Rachel's voice on the telephone had sounded flat and far away. The connection wasn't clear. He mentioned it and she made no comment, as if it didn't matter. He told her he would make a reservation for his car in the morning. Silence. Then, without any preamble, she told him that a letter would reach him in the morning.

He concealed his surprise at this breach of her accustomed behavior. He had no feeling of crisis, however; to write a letter to a tardy love was not a departure from love's ways. Rachel undoubtedly knew there was little chance of discovery. With all the mail pouring in for the bride-to-be, and all hands needed to keep abreast of it, nobody would have the time to be interested in a letter addressed to anyone else.

But he was profoundly sorry that Rachel had felt driven to write and remind him of his inattention to the woman who would be his wife—at least, and quite openly, his intended wife—as soon as the dust of Shelby's marriage had settled. He began to apologize for his busy week. But she interrupted to say, in a voice as dry as autumn leaves, "Don't apologize for the wedding. I believe in weddings. They should come before everything else, or everything else is nothing. But it's much too late to philosophize. I'll hang up now, if you don't mind. Good night, Clark, tomorrow, you'll have my letter."

He heard the finality of the click despite that second of hesitation when something affecting their future had been weighed in the balance. But nothing had been settled. He had said nothing he'd rung her up to say. Didn't she know that she hadn't asked when he would be in New York, or how they were to plan their brief holiday? Was her avoidance explained in her letter? Had she given him an ultimatum, set a limit to his patience? Marry me now or be my enemy?

With the end in sight and a new beginning in sight, why would Rachel, who had always been so predictable, let a few lost days scratch the immaculate surface of their perfect understanding? There was nothing to prove in punishing him by pointedly ignoring the purpose of his call. To treat their love as if it were one and the same with their lovemaking, to dismiss their tryst as if that was the surest way to bring him swiftly to one knee in penance with a proposal of marriage on his lips and a ring in his pocket for when she said "yes," was to squander the treasure of their mutual trust in a wholly feminine fit of pique.

For a moment she had seemed on the verge of recanting, or giving him equal time for rebuttal. Then there had been that negation, that "no" said to herself or to him, signifying some dark withdrawal from reasonable behavior. Always before when he had thought of this impasse he had turned his mind away from it in fear. Now, though, with the phone call, there was a new sense of urgency. He knew that he must act, however cruelly inappropriate the time and place. He would ask Corinne for a divorce before he left the island. The morning after the wedding he would ask her for his freedom, agreeing to whatever terms she might impose to punish him. With Rachel, and his practice, and the end of secrecy, there would be nothing more he needed for fulfillment.

In the summertime of the Oval, when screen doors replaced solid doors, and everyone saw everyone throughout the day, a closed door would only bring solicitous inquiry. He would have to leave Corinne exposed to whatever knowledgeable deductions were drawn from her altered look. The married, like the old, never know when they are next and cannot help but hope the plight of others postpones theirs. Many would sift through the ashes of a burned-out marriage, a few of them looking for a spark to rekindle it, but most of them looking for evidence of the other woman.

He drove home and got quietly into the twin bed on the other side of the room from Corinne. It was Corinne's bedroom, which he was sharing only because his room had been borrowed for two of their house guests.

Corinne did not stir. The evening had been lively, and she slept soundly, her breathing audible. He had not even looked at her, not because of any distaste, but because he had been filled with an obsession for Rachel greater than anything he had felt since the first tempest of possession. All through the night he had ached for her. He saw her in her nakedness. In his fitful sleep, he had dreamed of her in the dress that his daughter would wear at her wedding. In his dream, Rachel had been as he had once known her: young as morning, a graduate from a nursing school. She had had no seasoning, but her eyes had implored him to let her try, dissolving whatever resistance he might have mustered, and her soft, unslurred Southern speech, so unlike the careful brittleness acquired by Corinne, had completed his capitulation. Clark had been doomed from that point on because, while not everyone can see it, those who can know that there is no beauty like that of a brown-skinned woman when she is beautiful: the velvet skin, the dark hair like a cloud, the dark eyes like deep wells to drown in.

And yet Clark would not have hired Rachel if he'd known he was going to fall in love with her. It was not a calculated act. As young and expectant of life as she was, she was entitled to more than a married man could give her. He told himself that he was hiring her for a trial period in which she would have to prove her capabilities. What he was never able to tell himself was all the ways she reminded him so sharply, so powerfully, of Sabina, with whom he had had that sweet and unfulfilled encounter, from whom he had taken the trust and expectancy of a proffered heart and traded them for Corinne's empty vows.

Now, however, as he sat in the station wagon in the crowded gravel parking lot by the dock, he wondered if he would ever be free of the questions that licked at his brain like flames. He looked down at the letter again, and again he took it in, hoping that it had changed since his first reading.

Dear Clark,

In these long weeks without you, I've had time to do a lot of thinking about the past and the present and now the years ahead. I know the wedding has had to take first place in your mind in these last days of preparation, with all hands needed to meet the standard of perfection of the Coleses. The wedding has absorbed my mind, too, though for very different reasons.

I'm thirty-nine, and in December I'll be forty. Perhaps if I had already crossed that bridge and looked the same and felt the same as I had twelve hours before, I could think of myself as being only one day older instead of one year older, and the bond between us would still be secure.

I've tried to cling to that hope, but every day my doubts diminish it. Clark, a woman still unmarried panics when her fortieth birthday comes due. She knows, as I know that I know too, that time will not turn back, and the next decade I'll be fifty, and only God knows the number of my remaining years, with no children and no grandchildren to remember me when the counting stops.

My children were never conceived. It was my choice even more than it was yours. I did not want to bear a child who would have no legitimate claim to your name. Your love was total compensation.

When I turned thirty, you joked about my coming of age, and we both laughed. You said that I had grown prettier and only looked an inch or so older. It was my love for you that made my face glow.

A man in his forties and into his fifties is considered to be at his peak in any performance, business or bed, but a woman's ego is not treated likewise. That I was twenty when we met seems almost impossible. I was just out of my tiresome teens, out of nursing school, too, the top student in my class, ready to test my skills in the magic city of New York, so distant and different from my small hometown. It was a long-time dream come true. That I would ever be forty was light-years away from my thinking.

Then I met you, and how we met was as awesome as a miracle. I had never known or ever seen up close a colored man so self-assured and sophisticated. I fell in love with you instantly, but I tried not to let it show. My common sense told me that a successful and hand-some man with your charm would hardly be a bachelor. And so I confined my wishing to hoping that one day through you I might meet some ambitious young doctor who could use the encouragement of a wife who knew his field and would help him climb until he reached your height.

But the day that I fell at your door, I fell at your feet. And I knew that I was still a green girl helplessly falling in love at first sight, not yet a seasoned woman who could control her heart. Working with you and loving you and making love with you became my world. I was a grown woman who knew her own mind, or so I thought.

You've talked about asking your wife for a divorce when your daughters were married and their husbands had replaced you as their protectors. But too often the dream turns into a nightmare. I don't want to know if you might change your mind about marrying me. I've chosen to change my mind instead.

Tomorrow, when you receive this letter, I will be the wife of Jim Logan. Just the two of us before a justice of the peace. I'm sure Jim's name is not on the guest list of your friends, or on yours, nor is mine. Shelby's wedding will be totally unaffected.

Jim's been a city employee all of his working years. When he retires, his pension, which is adequate, comes due. As for me, I am hopeful that some doctor or hospital will find my years of experience worth an interview, and that the outcome will be satisfactory.

Jim's wife died two years ago. We met years before at bridge parties and became close friends. I rarely spoke of these gatherings to you because your disinterest in them was apparent and understandable. His daughters know me and are fond of me because of my affection for their mother. They are married themselves with young children. Their jobs and their families leave them little time to keep in daily touch with their father and his quiet way of life. When he asked me to marry him, I think it was with their coaxing, and maybe their coaching. If they knew about you, they knew I wore no wedding ring, and persuaded their father that the risk was worth the try.

I will sleep in my own bed, but he will not be unwelcome if or when he asks to come to me. He loved his wife. I can never take her place, nor can he take yours. He misses a wife's companionship; I need a wife's sense of security.

I do not regret the years we were together nor will I ever forget them. I have rewritten this letter three times and it always comes out the same way.

My best to you, Clark. I hope you will wish the same to me.

Rachel

Clark's hands trembled as he finished reading the letter. He suddenly noticed the quality of the air in the car—through the closed window on his left the sun's lancing rays seemed to shimmer before him. The fight thinned out the oxygen somehow, and he could feel a pressing on his temples.

Clark shook his head sharply, suddenly recalling why he was sitting in the ferry parking lot. Greeting Corinne's tiresome relatives, exchanging small talk, driving them to the Oval . . . it seemed at that moment absolutely inconceivable—he had to get out of there. No, he decided. He'd face Corinne's wrath. With that, he flipped the key in the ignition and began the drive back home.

CHAPTER THIRTEEN

*C*lark's car careened through the Oval. The two front windows were rolled all the way down, and the dirty wind rushing in clawed at his throat and scattered the papers that lay on his back seat—ledgers, receipts, a brown paper bag. He jerked the steering wheel to the left and guided the wagon—a source of pride, the first of its make on the Vineyard—up the gently sloping gravel path that ended in a semicircle in front of the kitchen door to the house. He took the path too fast and had to brake sharply, bracing his arms on the wheel as he did so. More unfamiliar cars were parked in the grass, more off-island visitors. Well, they could all go hang, he thought to himself. He turned off the car's engine and slumped down in his seat.

Then a curious coolness came over him, and as he

looked down at the letter lying in his lap, it seemed far away somehow, like a ship on the horizon, or a penny glinting at the bottom of a well. He took a deep breath and raised his head, and he did the only thing a Coles could do in his position: he pulled himself together. Here was a man born into the finest family Harlem had to offer, a man sent to the best New England preparatory school there was, a product of Harvard Medical School, a successful diagnostician, the owner of a brownstone on Seventh Avenue and 136th Street that was the envy of most, the owner of all he now surveyed, a sparkling blue house with glassed-in porches, set back on an immaculately tended lawn. Here was a man not accustomed to questioning his assumptions.

Clark had bought this property, the most coveted in the Oval, almost sight unseen. As successful as his practice was at that time, the house would still have been beyond his means, except that its previous owner, an old spinster, had died suddenly, leaving it to a faraway brother who was anxious to sell.

Clark would not learn until after the house was purchased that the spinster was Miss Amy Norton Norton. Her father had willed his house to her, well knowing that on his death the others would probably scatter to other resorts if their mates expressed a desire for a change; knowing, too, that his spinster daughter would always have room for them all, while they, because of marital pulls, might not have room for each other. That *this* was the house that only a generation later Clark Coles was to buy for his family was almost too perfect for Isaac to quite believe. Clark was sure that his father disapproved of their annual summer hegira, perhaps thinking that the whole enterprise was tempting fate, risking the wrath of an angry God who would not be amused by the indulgence implied by so much leisure time. Maybe Clark was right, for Isaac never did return to the island to see this incredible sight for himself, to the end too much a product of his generation, the generation of colored people that had not yet learned to take vacations, let alone own a summer house. But he had always recalled the Elysian summers of his boyhood to his sons, and Clark was the son who made real a dream his father never thought to have, the dream of owning a home on the island. And that by some happy coincidence it was the very home Isaac had summered in as a boy made it all the sweeter.

In the years before Isaac's death he grew more blasé about his son's vacations, but it always saddened him that one part of the story of his childhood that none of his family had time to remember was the role Miss Amy Norton Norton played in his life. She was the hand of God who had plucked him out of the Jim-Crow-riddled South and into a new life. So many whites had done so much to make the colored man's life miserable that it was all too easy to forget the miracle that was the migration of white spinster schoolteachers, women—mostly Presbyterian or Unitarian—who flocked to the South, giving up everything they had to teach a generation of newly emancipated children, most of whom had less than nothing. It would have saddened Isaac to know that Miss Amy Norton Norton's name would never be mentioned to his future grandchildren, one of whom was to be married in the ballroom in which Miss Amy had danced when she too was of marriageable age, though not of marriageable mind, having found no man whose name was worthy of substituting for hers.

As Clark thought about the ceremony that would take place in his house in less than twenty-four hours, a wave of bitterness washed up from within him. He had been too preoccupied with planning his upcoming life with Rachel to pay all that much mind to Shelby's wedding and its implications, outside of the formalities that it had been incumbent on him as father to dispatch in the past weeks and months, most of which involved his checkbook. But now where Rachel had been nothing but a hole remained, a gaping wound in his side that would never scab over. In place of that hole there had been a lifeline just a few hours earlier, an invisible cord that had always fed him, sustained him, no matter how far away he traveled. Without it, he felt himself transparent, insignificant, a shade of his former self. All he had left were his daughters.

A cool northern breeze blew through the car. It was such a beautiful day, Clark thought to himself grimly. He felt detached from his observation, the way he imagined an engineer might feel surveying a grassy knoll that was to be dynamited to clear the way for a road or a set of railroad tracks. A stillness in the air seemed to hum at his ears, and for the first time in a very long time it did not much matter to him what he did next. Clark had always felt a sort of perverse pride in the way his life moved from demand to demand, the way he stoically shouldered the weight of his responsibilities with his chin thrust out nobly. Now, though, when he considered the switchpoints and crossroads he had bulled through he had to ask himself what his life boiled down to.

What was his life, really, but a series of missed opportunities, a succession of situations in which he had waited too long to act?

First there had been Sabina, and everything since then was in a way a curse on him for never apologizing to her, never explaining. What explanation was necessary, though? In Sabina, he had never seen anyone more desirable as a woman; in Corinne, he had never seen anyone more desirable as a wife. She was everything his Brookline background demanded—she was fair, she would give him fair children, and her father was near the top of an honorable profession. No, his blood did not boil in Corinne's presence, no, she did not set his skin ablaze the way Sabina did, but were such base urges the stuff of lasting relationships? Perhaps not, but now, Clark mused, he had thirty years of evidence that their absence was no guarantee of happiness either.

And now Rachel. Clark did not know where to go from here. He had held the revered position of Dr. Clark Coles for so long, he had rested for so long against the cool pillar of icy imperative and thought that at the end of the day that would somehow be enough to keep the demons at bay, he had stoically borne the burden of his parents' expectations, but all at a terrible cost. Advanced social position did not come without an abnegation, an obliteration of the personal, the intimate, the hidden, the passionate. A balance had to be achieved, but that was a lesson learned at the expense of all too many of Clark's generation, a generation half afraid that all the insidious white stereotypes contained a germ of truth, a generation mired in the self-hatred that was bigotry's most monstrous crime, more damaging than a laundry list of physical indignities because it amounted to a mental rape, a theft of personal dignity.

Clark ground his teeth bitterly. Never to have a chance to defend himself . . . yes, fine, hard enough . . . but never to be able to say good-bye, never to win some sort of closure, however heartrending, *that* was the cruelest twist. Memories, images of the sweet, intimate moments they shared, danced in front of his eyes. He thought of obscure gestures of small, silent tenderness, tiny moments that contained within them an eternity, moments he had never shared with anyone before, and would likely not share with anyone ever again.

Clark opened the car door and stepped out onto the lawn. Perhaps it was too late for him. Perhaps he had passed his own personal point of no return long ago without ever realizing it. What was the word his pretentious friends so favored at cocktail parties? Karma?

It may be too late for me, he thought. But it might not be too late for my daughter.

CHAPTER FOURTEEN

$\mathcal{S}$helby looked up from her desk and put her pen down when her father strode into the room and closed the door behind him. He had a look on his face that she had never seen before. "Dad, what's wrong?"

Clark stopped short in front of her desk, his hands twitching at his sides. He turned abruptly and began pacing from side to side, his fingers restlessly drumming his pants legs until he noticed them and laced them together behind his back to subdue them. He stopped in his tracks and turned to Shelby, a storm in his eyes.

"Shelby, I don't know how to say this, don't know that I have a right to say it, don't know that it will make a bit of difference." He paused, flustered. "I don't claim to have been a wonderful father to my daughters—"

"Oh, Dad . . ."

"Let me finish," he said tersely. "—don't claim to have set a particularly wonderful example for you in terms of the institution of marriage. I know it must seem to you that Corinne and I are not as close as perhaps one might think we should be. And I'm not naive, I know that children have eyes, and ears, and a brain to read what their senses tell them. And so I know you're probably aware that your mother and I, we . . ." Clark was in agony. He despised human weakness, and he could neither believe that he was responsible for the words coming out of his mouth nor stop himself from saying them.

"Dad, I don't know what's gotten into you." Shelby picked up a seashell paperweight and placed it on the letter she was writing. She pushed her chair away from the desk. "But I'm getting married tomorrow, and I love you, and I love my mother, and I know full well"—she grimaced, thinking of the morning's argument with Liz—"that the fire died for the two of you some time ago. But why you would choose now to unburden yourself is, I admit, beyond me."

Clark drew himself up, a pained expression set deep in his normally impassive face. Just a few hours ago the idea of having this talk with his daughter would have seemed absurd, but now he could do little to quell the pain inside him that howled to be set free. "Shelby, Meade is a fine man. He is talented, and handsome, and decent, and you'd have to be blind not to see that he's devoted to you. I see how he looks at you, and if there had been anything but love in his eyes I would have throttled him long ago. But he loves you, I can't deny it; he does love you."

Clark walked over to Shelby's bed, Shelby following him silently with her eyes as he hitched up his pants and sat down. A few grains of wet sand still clung to his legs from his morning walk, and he brushed them off absentmindedly and watched them fall to the hardwood floor. Utterly uncomfortable, he looked like what he was: a father mightily unaccustomed to arguing with his daughter about affairs of the heart. Having in the past always assumed that Corinne would make their daughter understand all of the personal, feminine things she needed to, when she needed to, he found himself treading on dangerous ground. "Now when I was your age, if somebody had asked me what I thought love was, I would have told them. I knew what love was. Didn't everybody know? Right now, I might not be able to tell you how I would've answered that question back then, but I do know that I was a lot more sure than I am now. The fact is, sometimes I think romantic love is just another scourge put on this earth by the Lord, another measuring rod that no one thinks they quite measure up to, a simple idea that never seems to fit the two messy lives it's assigned to cover."

"Not to stop this fine sermon when you're on a roll, but what do your doubts about love have to do with me?" Shelby was growing more and more indignant. "You yourself admit you're hardly an expert on the matter."

"And you are, my sweet young daughter?" Clark raised his eyebrows. "You've never given the time of day to a single black man who's taken an interest in you." He stared at the wall.

Shelby drew her breath and scowled down at the edge of

her desk. Her throat felt too choked with her indignation to respond to the accusation she heard on her father's lips.

"But it so happens that the first white man who pays attention to you—"

"Stop it! Stop it, stop it, stop it!" Shelby clenched her fists and pounded them down on the shiny surface of the mahogany desktop with a resounding thud. "You take the prize." Her neck snapped back and she stared at her father. "I expect this from Meade's parents, but even they might pause a little before laying in the night before. How dare you?"

Clark's eyes narrowed. "This isn't coming out right. I just have to know the truth, is all. God knows what love means, but if this marriage is about love, then I won't say another word. But I've never seen you give your trust to a colored man, and I can't help but think that maybe that's because you saw in the one you know best a man who can't be trusted. And I've never seen you give your love to a colored man, and I can't help but think that maybe that's because the man who should be the most important man in your life never found time to show you the love he felt. And I've never seen you give your respect to a colored man, and I can't help but think that maybe that's some warped extension of this family's social snobbery. And if that's all true"— Clark's voice rose—"then I will do anything in my power to make sure this marriage does not happen."

The last word died from Clark's lips, and this final exhalation of breath seemed to take with it all the life he had left in him. His shoulders slumped like a defeated toy soldier's and he slowly put his face in his hands.

Shelby stared at her father in mute amazement. She had never seen him so broken, and an amorphous stew of pity, revulsion, and hatred stirred within her. As she pondered his words, the hatred won out. "I guess this is a thought that just occurred to you? Or did you think the whole wedding was one big joke, and you had to wait until now to make sure we were really going through with it?"

"I will not tolerate that attitude from you," Clark muttered, head still cradled in his hands.

"You what? But I'm supposed to let you tell me your heart, call my emotions into question, today of all days? I *know* my heart, damn you. I can tell love's deep roots from fear's shallow scratching. My heart's being pulled toward something beautiful; it's not recoiling from something ugly, unless it's you."

Clark looked up with haunted, bloodshot eyes. "You're sure?" he drove at her. "You're sure enough to gamble the rest of your life on it?"

In a flash, Shelby snatched her seashell from the desk and hurled it against the far wall, where it shattered into tiny pieces. "Oh, God, what is wrong with this family?" she screamed. "I know my heart. I do. I do." In one motion she flung herself out of her chair and toward the door. Clark rose up unsteadily to intercept her, but he was too late. The door slammed in front of him, and he slumped against it, spent.

CHAPTER FIFTEEN

$\mathcal{S}$helby pounded down the wide hall, her feet echoing in the stagnant air. She passed the open door to her parents' bedroom, passed the perpetually closed door to Gram's room, and slowed in front of her sister's room. She slipped into it quietly and locked the door behind her, breathing a quiet sigh of relief that Liz was still out with Laurie. She braced herself for the sound of her father's footsteps, but when after a few minutes she still heard nothing she turned and hurled herself onto her sister's bed. Only then did she allow herself to leak the slow, hot tears that she had been too proud to shed in front of her father. Drained and exhausted by the ferocity of the emotions Clark had unearthed, she soon fell asleep.

———

She awoke to the rattling of the doorknob. At first she could not place the sound, but when she did she braced herself for another clash with her father.

"Shoot," a distinctly feminine voice muttered from the other side of the door. "I *never* lock this door."

"Liz?" Shelby cried out softly.

"Shelby? Is that you? Open this damn door, you fool sister."

Relief and embarrassment swept over Shelby, and she quickly leaped to the door and opened it. Liz swept in, and Shelby closed the door behind her. "I've been looking for you everywhere, and here I find you skulking in my room. What's wrong with you? I thought you'd gone to the beach. Mom took a flock of cousins up island, Emmaline says, but she's back now." Emmaline was the Coleses' cook, an enormous ebony woman who was known on the island as one of its worst gossips. "Someone begged to be shown some local color, so Mother took them sightseeing . . . serves them right for asking. It apparently couldn't wait, not that people have anything else to do around here without Mom going to the ends of the earth to show off her island. Can you believe her?" Stopping to catch her breath, Liz turned to the window. "Listen to those pinkletinks go." Shelby looked out the window, through which she could just make out the spire of the Methodist camp meeting rotunda in the distance, one of the few direct reminders of the time when this area was known for nothing so much as its summer revival meetings. The sound of the birds filtered up from the lawn below. Liz didn't know what special quality these Vineyard birds possessed that made them pinkletinks, but pinkletinks they had been, for as long as she could remember.

"Liz, Dad and I—" Shelby began.

Liz waved her arms in impatience. "No, no, wait. Your news can't possibly top *my* news." A sly smile crept across her face. "You will never be able to guess the contents of my right pocket." She patted the right side of her shorts knowingly and raised her eyebrows.

Shelby couldn't help but smile at the look of pure mischief on her sister's face. "You're right, I can't. What is it?"

Liz shook her head slowly and ran her tongue over the bottom of her front teeth. "Uh, uh, uh. Not until you tell me you forgive me for our fight this morning. I was unfair to you, and it's been bothering me all day." The impish look on her face told a different story.

Shelby put her hands on her hips and rolled her eyes. "You know I can't stay mad at you, Liz. Besides, I only have the energy to quarrel with one family member at a time, and right now it's Dad. Do you know he—"

Again Liz cut her sister off. "Never mind, never mind. Tell me later." But the look in Shelby's eyes told her that the cause of her sister's mood was more than a summer squall. "Oh, all right. What happened?"

"Dad told me I was marrying Meade because I'm afraid of colored men."

Liz threw her head back and laughed merrily. "Heck, I could have told you that a long time ago."

"Liz, stop it. It's not funny. You're just as bad as he is."

Liz put her hands on her sister's narrow shoulders and

bent forward to stare her in the eye. "Now listen here. That old fool's probably just jealous because you're doing what he secretly wished he could. Mom's as close to white as it gets, but she's still not the real thing."

Shelby brushed Liz's hands away and turned her face to the wall. "You're awful. You don't mean that."

Liz frowned slightly. "No, I don't, but I can't say that it would surprise me. In a way it would make for a powerful symmetry." She grunted. "You were too wrapped up in your own world to see how jealous Mom was when I married Linc."

"Jealous? That's a funny word for it. She hated the idea."

"Part of her did, but the rest couldn't stand the fact that I was following my heart and marrying a dark man, something she herself never had the guts to do, and never will. She sees herself in me, the side of herself she was never honest enough to face. But I can't blame her—she had Gram and her mother watching her like hawks, making sure she understood that skin color was a direct barometer of virtue."

Liz and Shelby stared at each other, two sisters squared off inside a cramped, locked room. Liz leaned back on one leg, cocking the other foot up on its heel and swaying it raffishly. "But enough of all that. *That* is not what I came here to tell you." Impatient with her sister's indifference, she reached into the right-hand pocket of her shorts and pulled out a square envelope, which she dangled in front of Shelby's face like a piece of cheese. "Emmaline got this from GiGi." Liz and Shelby both knew that there was only one GiGi on the island—Lute's housekeeper. Emmaline was the only maid in the Oval who would have anything to do with her: snobbery among the help was just as virulent as snobbery among the owners, if not worse, and only the Coleses' cook, absolutely secure in her position as employee of the Oval's most respected family, would dare befriend the employee of such a rank outsider, and an obvious social climber at that. GiGi had confided in Emmaline regarding Lute's attraction to Shelby, and both approved, or at least they disapproved less of that idea than the idea of a mixed marriage.

Shelby snatched the envelope out of her sister's hand and tore it open, devouring the contents. She noticed with a small smile that on one line Lute had tried to spell "imperative" but had given up, crossed it out, and written "important" instead. She looked up with a grimace and handed the note to her sister. "Oh, Liz, this is ridiculous."

Lute had been stalking Shelby all summer, throwing himself down next to her and her friends on the beach, sidling next to her in the grocery store. She was never more than polite to him, and when her friends teased her she was quick to dismiss them with a scoff, but she had to admit she found his attention flattering, even if the idea of having anything to do with him was absurd.

Liz crossed her arms over her chest. "Oh, I don't know," she drawled, "I can think of worse things than getting love letters from a damn sexy man."

Shelby said nothing; at times like this she found her sister's brand of humor particularly intolerable. Lute McNeil, sexy? She didn't know whether she found him sexy or not, but she did know he made her uncomfortable, with his frank stare and the words that he had no right to speak to her but did. Her friends had long whispered to her about Lute's sleek good looks, and the way he sashayed about the island as if he owned it. Shelby saw what they meant, but if the truth be told she could never quite *feel* what they meant, about Lute or anyone else.

Sex was the source of Shelby's worst fears, her deepest misgivings. What was wrong with her, that she never felt swept away by desire the way the women always were in the sand-filled issues of *True Romance* that got passed back and forth on the beach? She had found men sweet before, and nice, and fun to be around, but where was the pounding of blood at her temples, the blind lust that was supposed to consume her? In moments of panic, she wondered whether she wasn't highly sexed enough, whether she was doomed to fall far short of Meade's expectations. She knew the stereotypes that whites held about race and sexuality—would Meade expect more from her than she knew how to give? She knew her fiancé so well on every other subject, but here she drew a blank: it was a subject they did not discuss. In part she had loved him for that, loved the tender understanding with which he had acquiesced to her wish not to consummate their relationship out of wedlock. But sometimes she couldn't help but wonder if he would be disappointed, and in disappointment turn away from her. A man like Lute could teach her, wanted to teach her; but Meade, sophisticated world traveler that he was, had been exposed to so many exciting women. How could she hope to hold him with her lack of expertise?

Liz gave Shelby a playful shove. "Come on, baby sister, what's wrong? This man's been after you all summer. Don't tell me you're finally starting to crack, the day before your wedding?"

"Liz, I'm so confused right now I don't know what I think. When I met Meade, it was his music I fell in love with at first. I'd never seen a man make sounds like that come from a piano, never seen a man *care* so much about sounds coming from an instrument. He played that thing like he was giving birth, and his fingers pounded into those keys so hard I couldn't tell one from the other. I felt like I was in church. But maybe that's just it. Maybe I'm marrying him because he's safe, because so much of his passion is poured into his music, and who knows"—Shelby paused and turned her confusion-stricken face up to regard her sister—"maybe because he's white." Shelby pushed past her sister and strode to the center of the room. Her back was turned to Liz, and from behind her sister could see the tension rippling through Shelby's shoulders. "Could it really be true?" Shelby whispered softly, almost inaudibly. "Am I really afraid of sex with the highly touted colored male—because of Mother's compulsion, because of Dad's infidelity?" As if a wall had been removed inside her, Shelby talked faster and faster, pouring all of her fears out at her sister's feet. Her eyes blinked furiously. She was not accustomed to exposing so much of herself to her sister, and though she felt purged, she also felt vulnerable.

For her part, Liz was secretly delighted to play the role of counselor in an area on which she thought herself an expert, having lived through the dark night of doubt that preceded her own marriage. She stroked her sister's hair soothingly. "Shelby, it all comes down to how well you really think you know Meade. No one else can answer that question for you. Because if you don't know someone all that well, you react to their surface qualities, the superficial stereotypes they throw off like sparks. Lute equals black, Meade equals white. But once you fight through the sparks and get to the person, you find just that, a person, a big jumble of likes, dislikes, fears, and desires. Trying to figure what a man is going to think or do based on the color of his skin will tell you as much about you as it will about him. Look at Gram. Until I married Linc and had the baby, I never thought of her as white, you see. She was just Gram. I still don't, except when her rejection of my child throws the fact in my face. You don't think of people you know as white unless they remind you, any more than you think of yourself as colored unless a white person reminds you."

"I do know Meade, as much as I need to. I mean, you always have doubts, but you can't marry a man on a trial basis. And outside of marriage, there are some things that we just can't know about each other."

"Well, how's it been with you and Meade so far? How close have you come?" Shelby's silence spoke volumes. "Not that close, huh?" Liz shook her head. "Huh." She went silent herself, scratching her cheek thoughtfully with one hand.

"Don't give me your huhs," Shelby said curtly. "Not all traditions are so wrong, and I happen to believe that if you don't save some intimacy for marriage then what's the point, really?"

Liz put her hands on her hips and emitted a snort. "I don't think there's anything wrong with your decision. It just wasn't right for me. Sex is important, and if Linc and I hadn't experimented a bit before marriage"—she laughed wickedly—"how would I have known that I wanted to marry him?"

"What are you saying—if you hadn't liked it you would have broken up with him?"

"I'm saying that what worked for me doesn't have much to do with what works for you. If we've learned anything from being sisters for twenty-two years, we've learned that."

Shelby sighed. She was tired of doubting, tired of being confused. She wished Meade were there right then to tell her that everything was going to be okay, to calm her with a glance, a touch, but he wasn't. He was only a few miles down the road, staying at an inn with his best man, a friend and fellow musician, but he might have been in Nepal for all the good he did her now. She stared at the scrawled note still resting in her sister's hand. Considered one by one, her encounters with Lute that summer seemed irrelevant. They had seemed like the shooing away of a dog pleading for scraps, the dismissal of a panhandler begging for spare change. Yet now that she regarded them as a whole, these run-ins congealed in her mind into a disquieting mass. She had laughed at his callow mockery of her impending wedding to a white man, but now it was as if the black bile he had poured into her ears had quietly trickled down to a secret place within her and festered there. Shelby knew few interracial couples, but those she did know seemed as happy as anyone. She had always assumed that, if two people were strong enough to fight through all the obstacles thrown in front of even the possibility of marriage, surely they could face its day-to-day realities. Lute's words to her, built up from here and from there over the course of the summer, had introduced doubts, doubts she did not want to accept but could not quite shake. Lute was cunning: he had discussed his divorces at length, always blaming them on the impossibility of interracial marriage. He had described in agonizing detail the torment that he and his wives were forced to endure day after day and week after week during the course of their marriage, until the combined weight of so much societal disapproval crushed their love into fine powder. "Liz, what if I don't have the strength to fight a war against bigotry every day of my life, for myself and for my children?"

"What if you don't?" Liz answered impatiently. "Do you really expect an answer to that question? If you're that worried about it, why don't you just pass?"

Shelby recoiled as if struck. "You have to be kidding."

"Why? You could, you know, you easiest of all of us. Don't tell me you've never thought about it. Meade has a hard enough road in front of him without taking on the cross of your color."

"Don't be a fool. And live my life in shame and embarrassment, always scared of being exposed? I think not."

"Come on, Shelby, don't be so naive."

"No, you come on, Liz. I would never do that to my children. What, so I lie to them, praying that they never learn the truth? Or tell them the truth, and force them to live a lie too, force them to listen in silence as their schoolmates tell nigger jokes? Not while I have a breath in my body. And how much would we see each other if I decided to pass?"

Liz admitted that the answer to that question was difficult. Shelby could visit her freely, but if Liz visited Shelby without her husband and child, it would be tantamount to denying them. She eyed her sister with both amusement and concern. She liked Meade a great deal, liked his wit and his daring and the fact that he was a little dangerous, that he drew Shelby out and took her places she would never otherwise have gone. A few years ago, Liz would have chuckled at the thought of her sister sitting at the bar in a smoke-filled downtown jazz club waiting for her boyfriend to finish his set, and there was something magical about the way that fantasy had been transformed so swiftly into almost mundane everyday reality. That Meade and Shelby could meet and fall in love at all encapsulated for Liz everything she loved about Manhattan. But if Shelby were succumbing to doubts of this magnitude now, then she owed it to herself to face them, for Liz knew Lute's type far better than Shelby, and Liz knew that whatever spell he had her in would burst like a soap bubble upon close inspection, but unless Shelby faced Lute, confronted him, saw him for what he was, then it would be too late. She would be married, and a nagging cloud of doubt would never entirely leave her. Liz looked out the west-facing windows. "Time's running out, little sister. Your man is waiting for you."

"You really want me to have a rendezvous with Lute McNeil the night before my wedding?"

"Why not? Go! Get him out of your system. Get over it. This is the last chance for you to explore your feelings, the last chance for you to be sure."

Shelby bit her lower lip and self-consciously brushed a

lock of her hair out of her eyes. Her father had shaken her. What *did* she have to lose? It would be nice to be able to tell Lute McNeil off, to defend herself, if only to put her own mind at ease. "Why not?" she asked, smiling nervously. "Why not?"

Liz nodded approvingly. "That's the attitude. Then you can take those vows full of self-confidence." She danced aside and waved Shelby past with a flourish. "Just try not to let the entire world see you."

"Thanks for the advice." Shelby walked uneasily out of her sister's room and across the hall to the staircase. Grabbing the banister, she shook her head. "I have to be crazy," she muttered to herself.

Corinne Coles's little finger absently swirled her vodka tonic. It had been an exhausting week, and her mind was a blank as she stared out into the twilight. She had not touched her drink in a while, although occasionally she would lift her finger to her mouth and suck on it pensively. She needed more ice; all of the cubes in her tumbler had melted. When the screen door to the kitchen banged shut, she turned her head sharply, in time to see Shelby running across the lawn, sandals in hand. Where was that girl going? Dinner would be ready before too long. She was glad in a way that the absence of Meade's parents had allowed her to dispense with the custom of a rehearsal dinner. One less thing to worry about.

Where was Clark? She'd barely spoken a word to him all day, what with all of the last-minute details that had to be attended to. He'd been surprisingly docile all week, even allowing himself to be pressed into service as chauffeur, but his patience might have worn thin, because he had been short with her today on at least two occasions. She mentally shrugged. Probably just impatient to see Rachel. It amused her to witness the hoops her husband jumped through every summer, the lies he spun about where he was spending the last two weeks in August. If the truth be told, she enjoyed the solitude, she told herself. Let him go off to be serviced by that whore. At the end of the day, he was still her husband. There was a time when Corinne hated Rachel; now she just pitied her. She only hoped she'd managed to keep her own various affairs more discreet: she knew that there could well come a time when the moral high ground would be a strategically important position to occupy. Lord knew it had been easy to be discreet these last few years. She liked her men young, and the older she got the harder it grew to find eligible playmates.

As if she needed the fact of her aging underscored further, her daughter would be married in less than twenty-four hours. Now that all the preparing was over, she had a chance to let that fact sink in. Corinne leaned forward unsteadily and groped for the ice bucket on the tray in front of her. She plopped a few cubes into her glass and brought it to her lips. Whereas in her eyes Clark had treated the impending ceremony as if it weren't altogether real, she had long ago resigned herself to Shelby's choice. She smiled grimly. Perhaps she deserved credit as matchmaker: she had raised such bitter objections to Liz's choice of mates that she could see Shelby's choosing a white man as the lesser of two evils.

Corinne actually didn't mind Meade, it was just that she

could never come to terms with the thought of a grown man playing a piano for a living. Shelby had tried to explain jazz to her often enough, but she still couldn't quite take it seriously. In her experience, jazz was for illiterate men of no repute who bugged out their eyes and bared their teeth. If Meade couldn't find a profession worth taking seriously, how could he take marriage seriously? Her lust for dark black men under cover of the night mirrored her repulsion during the day, and perhaps it was jazz's open, even cerebral flirtation with the dark side, its willingness to let go and improvise with mind as well as body, that explained it, when for Corinne the two had always been sundered by a divide too vast to bridge. Or maybe Corinne was just a product of her conditioning—no more, no less. Whatever the explanation, she refused to concede a shred of inherent dignity to banging on a piano like a monkey while a bunch of liquored-up or smoked-up or hopped-up junkies thrashed around at a Harlem rent party, sweating on everyone and everything and howling at the moon as if all good sense had escaped them. Corinne took another long sip of her vodka tonic and leaned back in her chair. No, she just couldn't see it.

CHAPTER SIXTEEN

*T*he shadows were lengthening when Shelby stepped onto the beach. Squinting her eyes, she strained to see down to the nineteenth pole, where she could just make out the vague outline of a figure lying recumbent upon the packed sand close to the water. It had to be Lute. Shivering slightly against the high wind blowing off the water, she strode briskly toward him.

No one was entirely sure how the nineteenth pole had become the accustomed meeting place of Shelby's generation of colored vacationers. They were a blessed bunch, Shelby and her friends, the first generation of all the generations since slavery to have no self-consciousness about being colored and, having none, they had nothing but impatience for the peculiar change that came over their elders in the presence of people whose faces were often no whiter, whose incomes were often no greater, whose fears were compounded of the same insecurities and rumors of war, death, and taxes. They were the first to question their parents' strictures, to chafe under the pressure of pursuing a career that came with a convenient, self-explanatory title, like M.D., or Esq., preferring instead to gather on this beach and talk of Africa, or of becoming engineers or diplomats.

Lute turned his head as Shelby stepped deliberately around a piece of gnarled driftwood. He was stretched indolently on a plaid beach blanket, hands behind his head, shirt off, muscles rippling in the dying sun. He smiled brightly. "I'm glad you came," he said softly. "Why don't you sit down?"

Shelby twisted her mouth into a grimace and self-consciously tugged down the tied-off ends of her gingham shirt. "I really can't stay for very long." Lute shrugged and turned over on his side to give her room on the blanket. Shelby sat down stiffly on its far corner, hands clasped unsteadily around her knees. Greedy gulls swung out over the beach, their shadows crossing on the sand in front of the two seated figures.

Lute began to coax her into a conversation, talking about nothing at first—about his business, and Boston, and his three little girls—real things, surely, but it seemed to Shelby that he talked mostly to form pretty sounds with his mouth, soft liquid words that fell from his lips like a song. As much as she resisted, Shelby found herself lulled by his words, soothed by the way they blended with the low rumble of the crashing surf and the muted cawing of the gulls whirling overhead. Lute scooped up a handful of sand and made a fist through which, contracting and releasing, he pulsed thin streams down onto the blanket between them. Scoop, squeeze, scoop, squeeze, until he had formed a small pile. Shelby felt a strange tingle at the nape of her neck as she watched his long, thin fingers at work.

How different Lute and Meade were, Shelby thought. Lute was a craftsman, a man whose life was dedicated to old patterns, old forms, forms he followed with remarkable precision—forms that Meade rejected out of hand. Meade was an artist, a trailblazer. He dreamed of the day when he would no longer need to work as a sideman in television studios and recording studios to support himself, the day when he could play in jazz clubs full time, clubs like the one in which he had first met Shelby, dragged against her will by her more adventurous friends.

Lute talked on, seemingly satisfied with her occasional grunt of acknowledgment. Shelby often wondered at how relaxed Lute made her feel when he was around, even though his presence always came as a nuisance. She supposed it was his sugary flattery, the almost plaintive way he sweet-talked her. Safe in the knowledge that Lute was too far beneath her to be a threat or even a serious consideration, Shelby's vanity could enjoy his absolute attention. Her mind wandered back to Lute's run-in with Meade the month before. Meade had made two extended visits to the Vineyard that summer: on his first trip Shelby had introduced him to the owner of Oak Bluff's most popular night spot, and he had offered to let him play the next time he was on island. Meade had eagerly agreed. The fee was nominal, and Meade and his band were used to bigger venues in New York, but that wasn't the point. On his next visit he brought a drummer and a bass player, both eager for the opportunity to cut loose and shake the kinks out before an audience less jaundiced, less blasé than the ones they faced in the city. That night in the club—actually little more than a bar—Lute had approached Shelby, had sat down next to her while she watched Meade play. Then too she had refused to look at him, giving all of her attention to Meade. It was the beginning of the set, and he was playing his part in a soft conversation between piano, bass, and drums. He always played gently at first, having learned that it took crowds a little time to get used to the idea of a white man playing in an otherwise all-colored band, but Meade was on fire nonetheless—a cold, cool fire; it was the only way he knew how to go on. A man who knew once said that jazz was a woman's tongue stuck dead in your throat, and Meade played as if to prove that man right.

In Shelby's friends' eyes, he did, but to the older Ovalites, ragtime, even when it changed its name to the less egregious word *jazz,* was still a dubious profession that provided no fixed income. But a fixed income alone guaranteed nothing: the fact that Lute's bankroll continued to increase did not increase his popularity with the older Ovalites who were the guardians of the past and the fierce protectors of the present. That his children were endearing was no saving grace for the other summer residents—unless his reputation for misadventures was full of holes, which they doubted. And indeed their misgivings were to be borne out.

Lute had no idea that the man onstage at whom Shelby

kept staring was her fiancé, but when he found out he assumed that explained her nervousness and her reluctance to talk to him. Between sets, Meade left his piano and came down to the table. He was clearly amused by Lute's presence, a reaction Lute was not used to and found slightly unnerving, as if he were part of a joke that everyone else got but him. Meade and Shelby chatted briefly about the last set, and that made Lute uncomfortable too, unaccustomed as he was to the free and easy exchange of ideas between a man and a woman. In truth, Shelby was delighted to observe, Meade had shaken Lute's self-confidence. Lute had competed with men for the attention of a woman on countless occasions, but never on a mental level.

"Hey." Lute reached across to Shelby and brushed her cheek with the back of his hand, jolting her from her reverie. "I don't think you're listening to me."

"Maybe you should make more of an effort to be entertaining," Shelby snapped, irritated at his presumption.

Lute threw back his head and chortled. "Oh, really? If I can't be entertaining, at least I'll be truthful." Turning onto his stomach, he propped his head up with one hand and regarded Shelby seriously without saying a word. The silence drew on until, just when Shelby felt forced to say something, he spoke. "Shelby, I feel something funny in the pit of my stomach when I look at you. It's a sort of hunger gnawing up at me." He spoke slowly, drawing the words out. "What do you think that is?"

Shelby stared straight ahead. "I wouldn't know."

"Would you like to?"

Shelby pushed herself off the blanket, brushing the sand

from her shorts. "I've heard enough cooing for one day, I think. You don't know me, and you never will." Shelby was amazed at the audacity of this man, this father of three who had to have better things to do than whisper sweet nothings into a woman's ear the night before her wedding.

Lute was unmoved. "I know you better than you know yourself. You think you know what you want, but you really have no idea. You think you've found what you're looking for, but I look at you and I see a woman who doesn't even know where to start. You're on the brink of turning your back on your family, your community, your race, all for some white-bread fantasy you don't half understand. You're beautiful all right, a long, tall, beautiful high yella drink of water . . . set to pour itself out on a desert."

Shelby had to smile slightly at Lute's cheekiness. "And I suppose you think you're some vastly preferable alternative?"

Lute shrugged playfully. "You could do a lot worse. Would you look at me? I'm tired of talking to the top of your head."

Shelby's eyes remained locked on his waist. She would not look him in the eye. "Look at me," he whispered gently. "I'm not going to hurt you."

For the first time, Shelby looked him straight in the face. Keeping his eyes locked with hers, he rose slowly, in one sinuous motion, until he stood in front of her. She took a step back, but she could not tear herself from his gaze. "You'd be miserable in that all-white world, you know that, don't you? You know what that piano man of yours is doing, don't you? He's slumming, that's what he's doing. He's just looking for something exotic. Oh, he's hot for you now, but once he has had his fill of your hot black blood he'll cool, all right. You'll see. Mr. Charlie's been doing it to our women since slave days—what's different now?"

Shelby poked her index finger in Lute's face, eyes flashing. "You're one sad human being, Lute McNeil. Not everyone looks at women like you do, like they're pieces of meat. Face it, Meade scares you. He's a better man than you in every sense of the word, and you know it, so you try to bring him down to your level. Small chance." Yet, for all Shelby's anger, something in Lute's eyes would not release her, and something in her skin denied her own words. She had willed her body to walk away from Lute a half dozen times, but each time she was snapped back as if on a short leash. She told herself she could not leave until she had told him off, until she had made him see how wrong he was, how myopic and self-hating, but something else pulled her back too, something darker. Lute was the first colored man she had met who treated her as if she were made of flesh and blood and not china. He was an experienced master, a man who'd had white wives and colored mistresses. He knew what women were made of. He knew the ground rules of intermarriage, and he knew what seeds of doubt to introduce, seeds that would germinate in evil flowers of regret.

Sensing Shelby's indecision, Lute pressed his advantage. He stepped closer to her, his lips inches from her brow, his bare chest heaving almost imperceptibly. The air had suddenly turned cool, and she felt goose bumps along her arms. It was as if the island had come to a standstill: the sound of waves crashing seemed to recede, and even the seagulls gliding overhead seemed to quiet their cawing, as if out of respect. The two bodies—one lithe, sun-blasted, almost bare, the other fair, willowy, trembling—stood frozen in place. "Open your mouth," Lute whispered hoarsely. Despite herself, Shelby obeyed. Slowly, even gently, Lute raised his right index finger to her parted lips and traced their outline. Shelby closed her eyes, wanting more than anything to pull away but rooted to the ground as if stricken. Lute lowered his face and brushed her bruised, pouting lips with his.

With a strangled cry, with some superhuman reservoir of will she did not know she possessed, Shelby wrenched her head away from Lute's and shoved him back with the palms of her hands. "No," she mumbled weakly, "I can't. I have to go. My family's expecting me." Head throbbing, she turned away.

Lute caught her arm and jerked her back around. "Wait. We need to talk."

"Let me go, damn you!" Shelby shrieked, her voice piercing the night air. She had lost her composure completely, and now more than anything else she wanted just to run away.

Lute blanched and dropped her hand. "At least tell me you'll see me again . . . maybe tomorrow?"

"I . . . maybe."

"Just say yes. Tomorrow morning, eleven o'clock. Here. You have to give me that. You have to talk to me. You owe me that much."

"I don't know . . . we'll see." Nodding her head vaguely, Shelby scooped up her sandals and moved backward, slowly at first and then faster. Finally she turned and ran up the embankment. She made it to the road without looking back.

"So it's agreed! I'll see you here!" Lute cried out after her retreating form. She did not respond. He clapped his hands together and laughed, and the sound was picked up by the wind and carried far out onto the ocean.

Della Connell (not McNeil, for by mutual consent Della and Lute had agreed not to live together openly until her mother died, knowing that if her mother found out about Lute she probably would die, but not before she cut Della off without a cent) stirred restlessly on a chintz armchair in the drawing room of her mother's elegant Back Bay townhouse. She was tired. It was late, and the room, lit only by a small porcelain lamp resting on a blackamoor table in a far corner, was dark. Even shrouded in darkness, the room maintained a light, ethereal feeling, due in part to its high arched ceiling and in part to the walls, which were glazed three shades of very pale lime green, toned in beiges, white, and *faux marbre*. She warily eyed the telephone that sat on the floor at her feet, beckoning her, challenging her, accusing her.

Della was amazed herself that things had come to this pass. Just a few short months before, she would have said that she and Lute had never gotten along better. But then he left for Martha's Vineyard with Barby, Tina, and Muffin, saying good-bye with promises to send for her once he settled in. First, the frequency of his phone calls, a veritable stream at his vacation's lonely beginning, had trickled down to almost nothing, until finally they stopped entirely. She had never expected him to return her letters (he could barely write), but when her own phone calls were met with impatience, then irritation, then cold indifference, she began to fear the worst, and two weeks ago her fears had been confirmed. He had called her at night, drunk and cursing, to demand that she grant him an immediate divorce. She cried and wailed and begged him to tell her why, but he refused, saying only that he no longer loved her, that he wanted a clean break. Something in his voice gave lie to his words, though, and she resolved to learn the truth. Then last week Lute had called again, angrier than before, demanding to know why no divorce papers had been forthcoming. He lashed out at her brutally, ordered her to fly with him to Mexico, where they could be served divorce papers easily and cheaply. He threatened to reveal their marriage to her parents if she refused him, and she could tell he meant it. At that moment she realized how desperate he was, for in causing her to be cast out and disowned—and surely his revelation to her parents could have only one irrevocable result— he would eliminate any hope he might have of coming into her family's money.

Lute had pushed Della to the wall. He had come close to breaking her, closer than she would ever let him see, but she was determined to fight back. She did not know why he was so desperate for a quick divorce, but in her heart of hearts she thought she could guess. He had met a woman, she was sure of it, and he had told her that he was already divorced. Well, whoever this woman was, she would be disabused of that lie soon enough. Pride was no longer an issue; Della had already sacrificed every scrap of dignity she might have once possessed for this man who had so effortlessly turned her love into ashes. She would see herself damned in hell before she'd let herself be thrown over by some nigger bitch, but first she would ensure her damnation on this earth: she would fly down to Martha's Vineyard and win Lute back from whatever woman was ensnaring him, for she had nothing if she did not hold him, the only man who had made her think beyond herself. She would face him, and remind him of the power she held over him. In the past, she had always found that she could hold on to Lute by keeping his nose pressed up against her world, giving him little glimpses of the sort of elevated life he had married into and would himself be privy to . . . in due time.

She had a seat reserved on a small plane, no more than a puddle hopper really, that left Boston at seven o'clock the next morning. She had his address; she would be at his front door by eight. The ticket in her purse was powerful evidence of the lengths to which Lute had driven her, for she was terrified of planes and had avoided them thus far in her life as if they were flying coffins. Fly to Mexico indeed, she thought. Lute had always tried to coax her into flying, and he had finally succeeded, but the flight was not going to Mexico.

Della picked up the phone and held it motionless in her hand. Then she slowly pressed it back down into its cradle unused, as she had countless times before. Enough, she thought to herself. Call him. She leaned forward in her chair, snatched at the receiver again, and dialed his number.

As the phone rang, she tried to compose herself, praying that one of the children did not pick up. She doubted it, though, late as it was. A click, and then a voice at the other end of the wire; it was Lute, and he was obviously in a good mood: his "hello" rang with childlike exuberance.

"Lute, it's me." Silence at the other end of the phone, and then Lute's voice again, the same and yet completely different, dry as dust, as if he had handed the phone to a nearby stranger. Inwardly, Della quailed at the change, but she steeled herself for the coming deluge. "Lute, I just wanted to let you know that I've decided to . . . surprise you. I'm taking a plane to the island tomorrow. I know this is last-minute, but I need a break from this wretched city."

The blast of invective that spewed into her ear made her physically wince. It was a bellow, an enormous uncoiling of rage. Never had she heard Lute so angry, so ruthless in his threats. "I'm . . . I'm sorry that you feel this way," she stammered mechanically, "but I am your wife, and I have a right to see you. It's not fair to keep me away, and I will not—" Another blast of bile interrupted her; she held the phone away from her ear and let him rage until he was spent. "Lute, I don't know why you suddenly hate me, what I ever did to you but try to help you, but if you want a divorce it will have to be on my terms." Della rubbed at the black circles under her eyes. "I will see you tomorrow, and you will look me in the eye, and you will tell me how your heart could have turned to stone. And if you can do that, I will leave you and never look back." Lute's voice in her ear lowered in key, shifting to a softer, more soothing pitch. He pleaded with her, cajoled her, begged her with every fiber of his being to wait, to hold off for just one week, so that he could prepare for her arrival with all of the ceremony it deserved.

But Lute's whimpering, conjuring up as it did visions of past days when power was firmly in her hands, only firmed her resolve. She spoke tersely into the receiver. "Lute, I will see you tomorrow morning, and that's *final.*" With numb resolve, she listened as he mounted another verbal assault, but before he could get very far she did something she had never done before. She hung up on him.

CHAPTER SEVENTEEN

$\mathcal{T}$he morning of the wedding broke cool and clear. The sun was still too low to burn off the sprinkling of dew that dusted the grass around Addie Bannister's cottage, and the only sounds that broke the still air were the excited voices of Barby and Muffin packing their bags for a day on the beach with their new-found friends from across the Oval and Jezebel's sniffing as she explored the treasure trove of smells that were to be found under the front porch.

The sun rose higher now, slipping through the stately trees in the park, dappling the grass with pale green places which highlighted the richer green of the shaded areas.

The Ovalites were coming awake. Baths were being run by the fastidious who bathed on arising, the conspiring odors of bacon and coffee were speeding up, the babies were beginning their demands, some cheerfully, some tearfully, and the women, with the wedding now only hours away, were groaning as they tried on girdles and high heels, and giving short answers to any query not concerned with clothes.

The onrushing sounds of the Oval filtered through the window to Lute's daughter's bedroom, and Tina awoke with a start, momentarily alarmed at finding herself alone in the room. As she drifted up from sleep into fuller consciousness, she remembered the outing her sisters had planned the day before. Barby and Muffin loved the beach, but Tina did not share their enthusiasm, preferring instead to spend her days in the orbit of next door's mother, even though it meant enduring the company of her two sons, Drew and Jaimie. Drew, twelve and dark-skinned, barely acknowledged Tina's presence, and Jaimie, nine and fair-skinned, acknowledged her presence by teasing and tormenting her. He was the devil of the family. He tried hard to be good so that he could get to ten, but he was so mischievous that his mother was sometimes afraid he wouldn't make it. Next door's mother seemed to favor Drew over Jaimie, but Barby told Tina that was just because she was afraid Jaimie would pass and break her heart.

Tina kicked off her sheets and stretched her stubby, nut-brown legs. She noticed that the sunlight pouring through the window was brighter than it usually was when she got out of bed. She wondered why, and she also wondered why her daddy had not called her down for breakfast the way he usually did. Shouldn't Barby and Muffin have come back already? Rubbing her eyes, she rolled out of bed and padded to the top of the stairs.

Peering between the banisters into the living room below, Tina saw her father sitting on the edge of the sofa, arms crossed. He was rocking slightly back and forth, and he had a funny look on his face that she did not recognize. "Daddy?" she cried out querulously.

Lute looked up, a tight smile on his face. "Good morning, sleepyhead. Don't you worry about anything. Everything's going to be just fine." He resumed his rocking.

Tina felt a twinge in the pit of her belly. Until her father spoke, she had been unaware that there was anything for her to worry about. She pressed her face between two wooden banisters and regarded him solemnly. "What do you mean, Daddy?" she squeaked.

This time Lute did not look up. "Nothing's going to stop this family from getting what it deserves," he said. "You're going to have a new mother soon to take care of you, and to make sure you grow up right."

Tina's face brightened and her eyes grew wide. Her little behind bumped up and down in excitement. "Really, Daddy, really? Who is it? Oh, tell me it's next door's mother." Tina held her breath.

Lute rubbed his nose thoughtfully. "Now, you know as well as I do that Mrs. Goodwin has a family of her own to keep her occupied. But Shelby Coles doesn't, and she's going to make you the best mommy in the whole wide world."

Tina had to bite her lip to keep from crying out. She did not know the name on her father's lips, but she knew whose name it wasn't. Next door's mother had been the source of all her happiness that summer and, until her father's words, the repository of all her hope. When next door's mother looked down at her, her smile was full and real, not like the smiles of the other mothers, smiles that never made it to their eyes, and barely made it to their mouths.

Suddenly Lute jerked his body around to the door; they heard the sound of a car turning up the gravel path that led to the front of the cottage. Lute snapped to his feet and faced the door. He clenched and unclenched his fists, leaning slightly forward on the balls of his sandaled feet as if bracing for the charge of an onrushing animal. His body was a coiled spring. A car door opened and closed, and the clipped crunch of high heels coming up the gravel walk grew louder.

"Tina, get to your room. Right now." Lute did not take his eyes from the door. Something in her father's voice brooked no argument. Tina scampered to her feet and ran back to her room, cowering behind the door and pressing her ear tightly against the painted wood.

Della had arrived. In the very act of coming openly into the Oval, she had sacrificed everything and turned Lute's own threat of exposure against him. She would have nothing now if she did not hold Lute. They were both fighting lost battles, neither one willing to admit their positions were hopeless. To Lute, Shelby was still no man's wife. To Della, Lute was still legally her husband.

When she walked through the door, Lute glowered at her ominously and pointed his finger over her shoulder.

"You should have told that cab to stay and keep the meter running, because you are turning around and going right back to the airport and taking the next flight back to Boston."

"I am doing no such thing," Della said haughtily, putting her bags down on the floor. "I did not risk my life flying to this accursed piece of sand just to turn around and leave. I am at least going to spend the night."

Lute raked his hands through his hair and pulled them down over his eyes. He stared at her through splayed fingers. "Why are you here, Della?" he growled. "Do you even know yourself? You think you can beg a man to be in love with you? Threaten him to be in love with you? Why don't you just let go, and get on out of here before you make more of a fool of yourself than you already have."

Della's face crumbled and turned ugly, the pure ugliness of a woman who has lost everything, a woman who has offered up all she has and been found wanting. She snarled at him like a cornered dog that had been kicked once too often. "The entire plane ride I kept thinking about the call you made the first night you got here. Remember those words? I believed you, you bastard. I waited for you. I'm not leaving this island until I see for myself what it was that poisoned your head so fast and turned your heart to ice."

Lute looked at his watch. It was ten minutes after ten. He had fifty minutes to get Della to the airport or all his lies about having already divorced her would float to the surface like drowned bodies. Della may have given Lute teasing glimpses of upper-class life among whites, but with Shelby he could share the same existence, only openly, with his daughters a part of it. He would not let this woman ruin everything he had worked for all summer, for himself and his family. "Della, please. You shouldn't have come. There's nothing for you to see here. Don't make this harder than it has to be."

"What's wrong?" she mocked, her blue eyes blazing. "You act as if you were ashamed of me. You mean you haven't been bragging on me? You haven't been telling this island all about me? Are they going to be surprised to learn that you are still very much a married man?" She bent over, picked up her suitcases, and started to walk to the stairs.

With a low snarl of desperate rage, Lute hurled himself at her. She dropped her bags and clawed at his face with her nails, furrowing long red trails into his cheeks, but he fought his way through her arms and pinned them to her sides. He stuck his jaw in her face. Sweat dripped from his nose. "If you don't get off this island right now, I'm going to *kill* you, you hear me? I am not messing around, woman," he hissed quietly, the veins in his neck bulging. "I'll kill you and feed you to the crows."

Della drew up a wad of spit and hawked it in his face. It hit his chin dead on and ran off onto the floor. "As long as I am still your wife, you have no right to order me around. How easily you forget who paid for this cottage. I'll leave when I'm damn ready." As she spoke, Lute ratcheted her pinioned arms back sharply, putting excruciating pressure on her shoulders. She drew in a sharp breath, eyes closed tight against the pain. "Let go of me, *nigger.*"

Releasing one of Della's hands, Lute hauled back and laid a brutal open-handed slap across her face. She partially blocked the blow, but it still struck her with enough force to send her sprawling to the floor, where she lay, momentarily dazed. With a savage effort, she raised her head off the ground. Flecks of blood mottled her lips. "I'll see you put in jail for that, chair maker," she hissed, her voice rising to a screech on the last word.

Tina huddled behind her bedroom door, her hands pressed to her ears, her mind blank with fear. This was the way Barby had told her Daddy acted with mothers sooner or later, but before now she had never believed her. The quarreling below grew more bitter. Tina did not know what to do, but she knew that she could not stay in the house a minute longer. She had been drawing a picture for next door's mother and could wish no better time to present it. The expected hug and kiss and gentle stroking of her hair would quiet her palpitating heart. Throwing caution to the wind, she opened her bedroom door, scampered down the stairs, pushed open the screen door, and sprinted out onto the lawn. Neither Lute nor Della noticed her run past.

Blind instinct guided Tina down the hill to the safety of next door mother's house. Tina knew she didn't want a mother named Shelby Coles, and she knew she didn't want a mother named Della. What she wanted was a smiling brown mother like the woman next door.

Lute stood over Della, arm raised. "Don't make me slap you again," he yelled. She wouldn't. He had slapped her more than enough, had beaten her into stunned submission. He snatched at the front of her blouse and jerked her teetering to her feet. Grabbing her bags with one hand, Lute shoved her toward the door. Sullenly, but without argument or resistance, she allowed herself to be led to his car, a midnight-blue 1949 DeSoto. He took her bags and put them in the trunk, and she stood unsteadily in front of the passenger-side door. Closing the trunk, he looked at her impatiently. "Get in," he snapped. "It's unlocked." She obeyed, slumping down in the soft leather seat.

Lute had used his car so infrequently that summer that he was worried it would not start, but the engine caught immediately. Pressing hard on the gas pedal, he backed out of the driveway with a lurch, then threw the gearshift into drive and shot forward down the grassy lane.

On this too-early hour on this day of all days the mother next door was totally unready for a visitor. Reluctantly, she had tried on the dress she had bought for the wedding months before, some sixth sense telling her that she had gained weight beyond its capacity to hold her inside it. Her doubt was soon borne out, and in her understandable agony she was totally unable to take time with a child who did not know what real agony felt like.

For the first time in their loving relationship, her voice was impatient; her face had no trace of a smile. "I'm very busy today, Tina. You go play with your sisters. I'm sure they're not far."

Mutely, Tina handed her the crayon drawing of a smiling brown woman, not knowing what else to do with it, and quickly left the house. Then, not knowing why—perhaps because it had watched her defeat, perhaps to release some unbearable pain inside herself—she picked up a fair-sized stone and threw it at her dog Jezebel to make her yelp in the same way next door's mother had made her yelp inside herself.

She was immediately sorry, and she ran after him— unseen on one side of Lute's moving car just as Lute suddenly saw the dog on the other side. Lute swerved to avoid the dog, and at the same time he heard Tina's wrenching scream.

As if underwater, he drove both feet into the brake, his mouth curled open in a moan of dumb despair. The wheels locked. The car slowed, but not enough. Tina's waiflike body soared up with eerie grace, head back, arms out. She seemed to hang in the air at the top of her body's arc, frozen against the soft summer sunlight flickering through the trees. Then, like a marionette with its strings cut, she fell to the ground.

Tina died in the nest of next door's mother's arms, too numb with pain to feel it or know she was dying, she who did not even know that children could die before they grew up to be like real people. Next door's mother held her to her breast, sobbing softly, clutching in one hand her crumpled crayon drawing.

Barby and Muffin heard the sound of their sister's scream from a distance and they ran to the road and to the sight of their father standing slack-jawed, arms straight at his side. They gathered around him and stared down at Tina. Muffin, young enough to still know what life meant but too young yet to know what death meant, stared in silent incomprehension, but Barby understood. Tina wanted a brown mother like next door's mother. Brown mothers hugged you a lot and made you laugh a lot. White mothers made you feel sorry and sad. Barby began to cry. "You know how to make her stop dying. Make her stop dying. Make her stop dying. Don't you love her? Don't you love her? She's my sister. I know it scares her to be dying. I don't know how to make her stop dying. Oh, Daddy, please." She looked at her father wildly. "You don't like mothers. You make them die. All Tina wanted was a mother and you made her die to make her stop saying it." She began to beat Lute's legs with both fists.

Lute started to cry. He had not cried since he was a child. At first he cried for his children, and then he cried for himself.

A crowd began to form around the car, and soon it swelled to encompass almost every family in the Oval. Suddenly, a woman pushed her way through the crowd from the edge of the road. It was Shelby. In a single glance, she absorbed the scene in front of her—Lute's white wife huddled inside the car, Lute with his daughters, two alive and one dead. A roiling fireball of rage and grief engulfed her, and she sank to her knees, hands drawn involuntarily to her mouth. The scales had fallen from her eyes. All of Lute's words about remaining true to one's race, all his subtle slurs, his sly digs, all were lies, pretexts. All of his deception and envy had led to this: the death of an innocent, a small girl who wanted a mother more than anything else in the whole world. Shelby could only thank God that it was not too late for her and Meade. Color was a false distinction; love was not.

From the porch of the Coles' house, Gram, Liz, and Laurie watched the crowd begin to disperse. Laurie began to cry, softly at first but then loudly. Her mother tried to quiet her, but she wailed on. Gram raised her head and studied the baby gravely. Then, without saying a word, she turned to her great-granddaughter and extended her hands.

Liz placed Laurie gently into Gram's wrinkled arms with a small, sad smile. Gram cooed softly as she rocked the infant back and forth, her finger tickling its dark chin. She felt the baby grow quiet in her arms, and she thought of Josephine, whom she had held the same way so many years before. She could not turn the clock back. She could not change the past or do much about the present. But she could spend the little time she had left on earth making things a bit better for the future. Liz put her arm on Gram's shoulder, and they turned away and walked back into the house.